THE SOCIAL HISTORY OF EDUCATION

GENERAL EDITOR : VICTOR E. NEUBURG

Second Series — No. 7

THE EDUCATION OF THE PEOPLE

THE EDUCATION OF THE PEOPLE

James Augustus St. John

THE WOBURN PRESS
1970

Published by
WOBURN BOOKS LIMITED
9 RUSSELL CHAMBERS, BURY PLACE, LONDON WC1

First edition   1858
New impression   1970

SBN 7130 0016 3

Printed in Great Britain by Clarke, Doble & Brendon Ltd.
Plymouth and London

THE

EDUCATION OF THE PEOPLE.

BY

JAMES AUGUSTUS ST. JOHN,

AUTHOR OF 'ISIS,' 'THE LIFE OF LOUIS NAPOLEON,' ETC. ETC.

LONDON:

CHAPMAN AND HALL, 193, PICCADILLY.

1858.

Dedication.

ordinary satisfaction the good already accomplished by your labours.

In every part of our mighty Empire, a strong desire for knowledge has been awakened : in the North American Colonies, in the West Indies, in South Africa, in Australasia, and in India, we observe indications of the growing vitality and power of the English mind.

But we must not suffer this circumstance to conceal from us the truth, that very much yet remains to be done. Ignorance is an enemy not easily put to flight. He has a stronghold in almost every mind, where, under various names and disguises, he maintains a perpetual contest with civilization. With this fact, experience has rendered you but too familiar. Even in places where you might have expected better things, you have encountered prejudice, party spirit, and opposition for opposition's sake. But your strong desire to elevate your humbler countrymen from the state of barbarism in which you behold them plunged, has enabled you to defeat and triumph over your adversaries.

Approving conscientiously all you have done for the enlightenment of the Industrious Classes of this

Country, I have experienced the desire to effect something also in furtherance of the same design. For
this purpose I have studied carefully the state of the
Country, and ventured to throw out such suggestions
as appeared likely to be useful at the present time.
Of my motives I am sure you will approve, and
I am not without hope that you will consider what
I have written, calculated to advance in some degree
the cause of Education.

I have the honour to be, Sir,

With profound respect and esteem,

Your obedient, humble Servant,

JAMES AUGUSTUS ST. JOHN.

13, *Grove End Road, St. John's Wood.*

CONTENTS.

CHAPTER I.

THE OBJECT OF EDUCATION.

CHAPTER II.

THE DOMAINS OF IGNORANCE.

CHAPTER III.

PREVALENCE OF SUPERSTITION.

CHAPTER IV.

OUR OWN HISTORY AND INSTITUTIONS.

CHAPTER V.

POETS, NOVELISTS, NEWSPAPERS.

CHAPTER VI.

PHYSICAL SCIENCES, IDEA OF GOD, SELF-INSTRUCTION.

CHAPTER VII.

GEOGRAPHY.— DIFFERENT RACES OF MEN.—DISTRI-
BUTION OF PLANTS AND ANIMALS.

CHAPTER VIII.

PHILOSOPHY OF EXTINCT RELIGIONS.

CHAPTER IX.

INFLUENCE OF RELIGION ON EDUCATION.

CHAPTER X.

THE AFFECTIONS AND DOMESTIC VIRTUES.

CHAPTER XIII.

EDUCATIONAL RATE.

CHAPTER XIV.

AGRICULTURAL SCHOOLS.

CHAPTER XV.

SCHOOLS OF EMIGRATION.

CHAPTER XVI.

STUDIES OF EMIGRANTS.

CHAPTER XVII.

MECHANICS' INSTITUTES.

CHAPTER XVIII.

INFLUENCE OF THE UPPER ON THE LOWER CLASSES.

CHAPTER XIX.

USE OF THE ARTS IN EDUCATION.

CHAPTER XX.

THF STUDY OF LANGUAGES.

CHAPTER XXI.

VIS INERTIÆ OF THE POOR.

CHAPTER XXII.

EFFECTS OF THE DIFFUSION OF KNOWLEDGE.

CHAPTER XXIII.

STUDY OF THE SOCIAL SCIENCES.

CHAPTER XXIV.

THE SOCIAL SCIENCES (CONTINUED).

CHAPTER XXV.

TENDENCY OF CIVILIZATION.

Page

EDUCATION OF THE PEOPLE.

CHAPTER I.

THE OBJECT OF EDUCATION.

THE first question we should ask ourselves, when we
form the design of imparting knowledge to the
people is, What object have we in view? Do we
merely desire to convert them into useful instruments
of industry, or, elevating our views to the level of

morals, politics, and religion, to render them better
in their social relations of parents, husbands, wives,
children, better citizens and better Christians ?

Many persons of station and influence among us are
beginning to be actuated by a strong desire to do something for the improvement of the masses.   In Parliament, and out of Parliament, they exert themselves,
make speeches, deliver lectures, and subscribe money,
in order to give an impetus to the cause of education.
But the effect produced has not hitherto been pro-
portioned to the efforts made, because the friends of
knowledge are not agreed about the means of imparting it,—some advocating one plan, some another.

There are those who regard religion as all in all,
while others contend for a mixture of secular instruction. Many lay stress exclusively on the study of the
physical sciences, while an equal number perhaps are
eager to force the popular mind into the track of literature, the fine arts, and other analogous pursuits;
which proves, that the upper classes in this country
do not generally understand the subject of education,
obviously because their own has been imperfect.

Even when our minds have been subjected to the
most extensive range of instruction, very few of us
are enlightened respecting the means of rescuing the
great body of mankind from the slough of ignorance.

Men otherwise remarkable for the largeness and cor-
rectness of their views, have often doubted whether
or not the people ought to be educated at all.　But
when we have surmounted this question, and determined within ourselves that nature requires all men's
minds to be furnished with moral and religious principles, and to be familiarized with those facts and
processes, an acquaintance with which is necessary,
to enable them properly to perform their duties in
the several stations in which they are placed, we still
experience extreme difficulty in settling how this is
to be accomplished.

Among those who take the greatest interest in
popular education, some, as Mr. Baines, Lord Robert
Cecil, Mr. Henley, and Mr. Hadfield, contend that
the progress of the people is extremely satisfactory.
Lord John Russell, Sir John Pakington, Mr. Cobden,
Mr. Bright, Mr. Gibson, Mr. W. J. Fox, Mr. Ewart,
the Dean of Hereford, and many others, look upon
the actual state of things with dismay : they maintain
that the amount of ignorance still existing among
the people of this country is incalculable, and they
attribute to it very much of the crime and misery
we witness on all sides.

Professor Blackie, a competent and liberal judge,
draws a very discouraging picture, even of the high-

est education in Scotland; while there are not a few who dispute the educational efficacy of our English Universities, which turn young men out into the world, with little or no knowledge of its actual state, or the wants of the existing generation.

These diversities of opinion perplex the Legislature, and prevent the passing of such measures as might otherwise diffuse light over the country. While the physicians are disputing about the best means of cure, the neglected patient is in agonies. Our differences however prove our ignorance. If we understood the matter better, we should be more agreed.

I do not, because I write this book, pretend to be wiser than my neighbours; but having thought a good deal upon the subject, and arrived on many points at certain conclusions, I consider it my duty to lay them before the public. Every member of the community has an interest in its welfare; and if he imagines himself able to do any good, he ought not to be blamed for making the attempt, even should his ideas turn out to be of little value.

A philosopher once said, " If I had the supreme direction of a political community, I should care little who made the laws, provided I had the management of education." But philosophers themselves are occasionally mistaken. To educate a community is

no easy matter. In the first place, we generally form
very false ideas of children: because they are weak,
and cannot resist our authority, they appear to be
docile, while perhaps in reality they are the very
reverse; they listen to what we say, they commit to
memory what we order them, they conduct themselves upon the whole as they are bidden ; but what
we are really aiming at is, not so much to regulate
the proceedings of those children, as to influence the
conduct of the men and women into which they are
some day to ripen. While we appear to be dealing
with the acorn, we are really thinking of the oak.

It is comparatively easy to rule those frail organi-
sations, with delicate complexions, small limbs, and
flaxen hair; but when time shall have furrowed the
cheek, darkened the locks, and developed the limbs
into powerful dimensions, will their actions be con-
formable to the maxims inculcated in childhood? As
the frame grows, the reason and the will grow also,
the passions acquire strength, and the whole being
assumes a new character. Then comes the trial of
education. If it has been good, it will have implanted some principle in the soul which nothing
can wholly subdue, which will defy events, circumstances, the influence of friends and enemies from
without, and the promptings of passion and appe-

tite from within. The individual may seek to escape from this internal monitor, to drown its voice amid the siren sounds of pleasure, to silence its upbraidings amid the tumult of business; but in the morning, in solitude, in the stillness of night, it will come to us, and pass judgment on our conduct, and terrify us and make us tremble, and compel us to retrace our steps towards those paths of pleasantness in which alone it from the first assured us that happiness was to be found. To accomplish this is to educate.

Since this can only be done by moulding the minds of children from the cradle, some appear to imagine that the state of the existing generation is hopeless. But in intellect, as in religion, there is a second birth. A man, whatever may be his age, is born again to the life of the soul, when he first begins to feel the want of knowledge. The infant draws its first breath with pain, but the first breath the mind draws is beyond expression delightful.

When we go about the streets, when we observe and listen to the crowds that pass us, we cannot fail to be struck by a thousand manifestations of ignorance. All improper conduct, all unseemly language, all harsh, coarse, and savage tones of voice, are proofs of the absence of education.

But if we proceed farther, and penetrate beneath the surface of society, we shall discover still stronger demonstrations that healthful and prolific knowledge is not very widely diffused. Few indications of this fact are more painful than the general prevalence of indifference. The majority obviously believe that the real object of education is, not to kindle, but to put out the great fire of life, which we denominate enthusiasm. To feel a deep interest in what we hear, to be susceptible of strong emotions, to sympathise keenly with suffering, to be eager to soothe, relieve, and comfort the afflicted, are regarded as signs of inferior breeding.

From notions like these the actual condition of society must speedily divorce us. Circumstances will compel us to remember that we are men, and that as such we have a great deal of work to do in this world.

Some cause, with which perhaps we are not acquainted, has begun to put the masses in motion. Some divine breath has breathed over the dry bones, and bid them live, and they are putting forth signs of life. Of this social resurrection we cannot, if we would, remain ignorant. The great body of society is acquiring intellectual life, which, according as it is matured, will blossom into good or evil. Nearly one thousand Mechanics' Institutes exist already, and

the number is fast increasing. Through these institutions knowledge will be conveyed to men of all
ages, and this knowledge must bear stamped upon it
the impress of religion and liberty, or it will hardly
be productive of much good to mankind.

But, although the process has commenced, the
domains of ignorance are still widely spread. Altogether the inhabitants of the British empire amount
to little short of two hundred and forty millions,—
nearly one-fourth of the human race,—and out of
these, how many can truly be said to be educated?
Knowledge is a trivial thing, unless it teach a man how
to live and how to die.   To live, is to be able to make
the most of all the circumstances which surround us;
to create for ourselves a field upon which our idiosyncrasies, intellectual and moral, may develope themselves independently, to ascertain exactly our own
worth and the worth of others; and to be able, by
the exertion of mental energy, to vindicate to ourselves the place we ought to occupy in the world.

But if this be education, how few are there who
possess it!   Generally knowledge precedes or accompanies property.   Here at home, out of the twenty
millions who inhabit England and Wales, fewer than
five hundred thousand have an income of one hundred a year; and if we look abroad, to North America,

to Africa, to Asia, and to Australasia, how infinitely small is the number of those who, owning the British sway, are gifted either with the wealth of the body or with the wealth of the mind.

To conquer, however, is to undertake all the responsibilities of government, among which the duty of imparting knowledge is unquestionably not the least.

By taking men under our rule, we practically say to them, Submit to us, and we will direct you into the path of prosperity, instruction, happiness; we will teach you what it is to be men; we will elevate you from the condition which rendered you inferior to us in arms, to an equality with ourselves; we will remove from your eyes the scales of ignorance, and enable you boldly to look the highest of your fellow-creatures in the face, and to share with us, if you please, those divine truths which bring a man into holy communion with his Maker.

I say, we undertake all this, when we enlarge the circle of our dominions, and admit new tribes and nations into political fellowship with us. But when we follow the glitter of the British standard over the globe, what is it that we behold?

CHAPTER II.

THE DOMAINS OF IGNORANCE.

The Domains of Ignorance.—Worship of the Ministers of God.—
The Gheber.—The Hottentot.—The Savage of the Australian
Wastes.—The Devotee of Kali. —The Hindoo Mother.—Sacrifice
of the First-born.—Extent of the present aim of Education.—Pre-
valence of Ignorance around us.—Incentives it supplies to
Crime.—War between Poverty and Property.—Numerous Classes
of Malefactors.—Social Horrors.—The Genesis of hardened
Guilt.—Terrible Fascination of Crime.—Mental Condition of the
Criminal.—Vast Social Purgatories—Public apathy.—Multiplica-
tion of Juvenile Delinquents.—Self-delusion of the Country.—
Humanity and Riches.—Fear of the Spread of Knowledge.—Duty
of the Upper Classes.

PLACE yourself where the land, shelving down suddenly with strange beauty, meets the tropical ocean.
Sand thrown up, like drifts of gold-dust, by the wind,
fringes the grass. There you behold a man, draped in
flowing costume, standing still as a statue. His face
is towards the East, where the pearly, purple, crim-
son, and saffron rays, surging up and intermingling,
foretell the approach of the sun.

He watches these indications with religious awe;
and the moment the golden disk appears above the

tremulous ocean, he is warmed into adoration; he folds his arms upon his breast, he kneels, he bows down his forehead to the earth; and forgetting the Creator, who lies hidden from mortal sight in the depths of infinity, he worships the visible splendour of his minister.

He is a British subject.

Again, you behold a figure, black as ebony, emerge from a mass of stunted brushwood, and approach the shore. He is all but naked. His hair is frizzled, his forehead retreating, his nose flattened to his face, his eyes are round and meaningless, his lips thick and projecting. He saunters along in listlessness, bordering upon complete apathy. Suddenly he sees something upon the beach, and all his latent vitality is awakened in a moment. It is a dead whale. He screams with joy; and having collected together a number of his friends, rushes towards the prize, and climbing up the side of the sweltering carcass, he seats himself, draws from his girdle a large knife, and prepares for a feast. Presently he is surrounded by heaps of green, ill-odoured and rancid fat, almost converted by the sun's vertical rays into oil, upon which he gorges to repletion. Stupified and half drunk with animal fumes, he retreats to some hole in the rocks, or in the earth, to sleep.

He is a British subject.

Again, look yonder, where, upon a burning flat, a dusky human creature, naked as at the moment he was born, creeps along lazily with a boomerang in his hand. He has no home, no wife, no child, no provision for the morrow. The soil beneath him half fire, half dust, scorches his feet; the sun from above parches and cracks his skin, and would strike him dead, but for that mass of hair which, matted with filth and peopled thick with vermin, protects what little brains he has. At length, as he strolls along, he perceives among the stones some limb of a sheep. Accustomed to carrion, he falls to at once, and never pauses until he has picked it to the bone.

What ails him now? His whole frame quivers with agony, his eyeballs roll, foam covers his lips; he falls upon the earth, uttering the most fearful groans. The mutton had been poisoned.

He is a British subject.

You stand in a small opening in the midst of an interminable forest. Between the trunks of huge trees you behold the grand pageant of day sinking slowly behind the horizon line, one flush of light fading after another, until the last lingering ray disappears. The sky above you has become one vast black concave, studded with points of fire.

Observe that solitary man; what is he doing there? He is kindling a torch, which when lighted he sticks upright in the fat earth. The red fitful light streaming through the glade falls upon a hideous colossal image of black stone. Moans and sobs are heard, and the man, apparently directed by them, proceeds to a clump of bushes, from beneath which he drags forth another human being, tightly bound with cords. His face is wild with fear; he implores for mercy in deep guttural accents; his eyes are turned up in piteous supplication. But the other man heeds him not. On the contrary, he pulls him on to the foot of the image, he stretches him on a flat stone, he draws forth a knife, and uttering certain formulæ to the black image, he plunges the knife into his throat. The victim struggles, and would speak, but the rush of the life-blood stops his utterance. The other now stoops and laps the purple gore, before it has time to sink into the earth.

He is a British subject.

We stand by a mighty river, which rolls its glad beneficent waters towards the ocean. All around us is picturesqueness and beauty. The banana showers its gigantic foliage towards the earth; the palm-tree quivers and droops its feathery leaves above; and a thousand parasites literally canopy the forest with flowers of all hues, yielding fragrance to the breath of every passing wind.

A woman, slender, graceful, and gentle, issues forth from beneath the palms. She has a baby in her arms; it is her first-born, the child of many prayers. She caresses it, she kisses it, she sheds tears over it, as if it were part of her own soul. She approaches the river, and gazes on its multitudinous waves. Presently she perceives close to the shore something black and grizly ascending slowly out of the water. It is the snout of a sea-monster, that by degrees shows its whole head, and opens its yawning jaws, which expand there dark and fearful as hell. The gentle mother presses her babe to her breast, kisses it wildly, fiercely, then disengaging it suddenly from her embrace, flings it with a mad shriek to the gaping monster, who disappears with it beneath the ripples. Having performed this act of piety, the mother returns to her home in the full belief that she shall be blessed with a numerous progeny.

She is a British subject.

Is it meant that the humanizing influence of education should be extended to those remote portions of the empire in which the originals of the above pictures are to be found? Not yet: there is ignorance enough within the boundaries of our own land to task for many years to come the utmost energies of the friends of knowledge. Unhappily we need not go to other hemispheres in search of savages, who, upon very slight temptation, would perpetrate the worst of crimes.

To reconcile ourselves to this state of things, we call actions by soft names, which, if invested with their proper appellations, would make our civilized country appear a very pandemonium in our eyes. We live in the midst of a perpetual social war. Thousands and tens of thousands who have retreated or been driven beyond the pale of legitimate citizenship are encamped among us, and devote every hour of the day and night to the invention or execution of stratagems against property and life.

To delineate the varied forms of crime would be to write an Iliad of social miseries, to lay bare horrors supposed not to exist out of hell,—the lives of men delighting in guilt, apparently for guilt's sake, glorying in their own corruption, and exercising all the arts of an infernal ingenuity to corrupt and destroy others. There is no form of treachery or cruelty which we do not see practised hourly. Parents beat their children to death, or thrust them naked into garrets or cellars, to perish by the inclemency of winter, or turn them loose into the streets to study and live by crime. Mothers sell their daughters to shame, or stifle their infants, or abandon them to perish by neglect. Plenty elbows want out of the streets; respectability derides poverty. When guilt is to be expiated by death, myriads throng together to witness the separation of soul and body, the contortions and writhings of pain, the twitching limbs, the blackened countenance; and men and children, accustomed to dishonesty, laugh, joke, and pick pockets under the gallows.

After a certain number of years, when the soul has been sufficiently steeped and tempered in evil, it appears to be placed beyond the reach of human sympathy, and to be inaccessible to reason. All the logic in the world would fail to convince some men that honesty is the best policy. They have tried all the arts of honesty and dishonesty, and prefer the latter. They afford them all the excitement of war; the silent march by night, the stratagem, the ambush, the lying long in wait for the enemy, the storming of strong places, the creeping into fortresses by stealth, the hand-to-hand encounter, the prolonged struggle, the bloodshed.

Then, when the hands have been made red, follows another series of incidents, the interest of which is of a far more terrible nature. The murderer finds himself in the position of Ishmael, his hand is against every man, and every man's hand is against him. He feels there is a brand upon his soul, and fears that the reflection of it may appear also upon his forehead, and, in the words of Cain, lest every one who finds him should slay him. He moves about therefore in perpetual dread. He has passed the moral Rubicon, and feels that there is no more pardon for him in this world, or perhaps in the next. Under this demoniacal persuasion he becomes tenfold more a fiend than before, and plunges into every species of loathsome sensuality, to blunt the sting of conscience and obliterate the remembrance of guilt.

Here and there, over the face of England, there are dens of vast dimensions, into which society thrusts villains like these, either till the quibbles of the law let them loose once more upon the community, or till the hangman dismisses them to their final account. Nearly all our great cities have their atmosphere tainted by these hideous abodes, the guarding of which converts large classes of men into the lacqueys of malefactors.

Yet we persist in deceiving ourselves respecting the true cause of these social phenomena. Too frequently we do not even give ourselves the trouble to inquire. We go on repeating the fact, that seven

or eight thousand children are yearly added to our
criminal population; that our streets are crowded
with juvenile vagrants, who are fast preparing to gra-
duate in crime; that our gaols are full to overflowing;
and that we are under the necessity of discovering
some spot in another hemisphere upon which we may
pour the incurable guilt of our own land.

How it has happened that we are reduced to these
straits, is what we shrink from explaining to ourselves.
We have learned to say by rote the responses of the
social catechism, and mutter day after day, and hour
after hour, that we are the wealthiest as well as the
most moral people in the world ; that our industry
and commerce are perpetually increasing; and that
our faith, our language, our civilization are diffusing
themselves over the most distant parts of the globe.
But if we possess greatness in a political point of view,
we are not by any means socially happy. Everything among us is in a whirl of excitement. Mere
humanity is accounted nothing. To claim our respect,
it must come to us accompanied by property, by
social position, by refinement, by polish, by knowledge, by energy. Without all these a man is nothing.

It has been said that everything is useful in a great
community, ignorance as well as knowledge. At any
rate we have a great demand for ignorance in this part

of the world. The notion is prevalent that knowledge in the lower orders may be found troublesome, and that when obedience is required, ignorance is the best security for its existence. No doubt a man whose mental powers have been developed requires to be treated as a rational creature. He must be led, not driven; and, in order to lead him, the upper classes must make greater proficiency in the art of influencing reasonable and thinking men.

It is some approach toward a better state of things to make the humble classes feel that we are concerned about them, that we are anxious to teach them something, that we want to raise them in the social scale. If we set about this task in an awkward manner, the poor will still give us credit for our good intentions; they will perceive that we desire to benefit them, and, though our efforts should often result in failure, they will still take our solicitude kindly.

But we must not let them suppose that we have any other motive for doing what we do, than the general desire to improve the condition of our country, of which they form so great a part. If education be regarded as a mere measure of police, the poor will naturally cherish hostility against it. They will persuade themselves that we always secretly contemplate them as criminals in prospect, and that

our whole anxiety is concentrated upon the preser-
vation of our own riches, and not on the amelioration of their manners, or the improvement of their
condition.

CHAPTER III.

PREVALENCE OF SUPERSTITION.

If we could draw out all the ignorant, and marshal them before us on a plain, we should certainly be alarmed by the prodigious difficulty of enlightening their minds. Our alarm would be increased, if we went from individual to individual, and examined the various forms and phases assumed by ignorance. We talk glibly enough of the responsibility of Governments, and of all those who are placed in authority over men; but if we really felt the weight of that responsibility, we should tremble at the state of mental

darkness in which our negligence has suffered a majority of our fellow-creatures to remain for ages.

It may fairly be doubted whether the savage races
of the earth equal many Englishmen in moral and
religious ignorance.   In the forest or the desert, Nature herself undertakes and performs a part of man's
education.   The vast phenomena of the universe, exhibiting infinite power in action, which he is soon
led to contrast with his own weakness, compel him
to recognise the existence of a God, and, from this
recognition to worship, the step is short.   There is,
accordingly, no savage without religion; but on the
outskirts of civilization men sink much lower than
the savage state.   Toil, incessant and monotonous,
converts them into mere machines.   Blinded by the
sweat of their own brows, they do not and cannot
look up to heaven. The highest thing they raise their
eyes to is their employer, upon whose nod they depend for bread.   As soon as their eyes open in the
morning, they alight either upon the implements of
labour, or upon their coarse and scanty food, or upon
the squalid faces of their wives and children, in rags,
ignorant, hungry, and discontented like themselves.
From that moment, until the day is closed, they work
with little or no intermission; and then, weary, hungry,
dejected, and stupefied by unbroken exertion, they

either sink into wretched hovels to sleep, or repair
to some den of low and degrading debauchery, to
waste the little money at their disposal in brutalising
themselves still more completely. Their wives and
children in the meantime share fully in their degradation.

It can therefore be matter of little surprise, when
we lift the veil from their inner nature, to find it
inhabited by monstrous forms of superstition. Civilization does very little towards extirpating such
chimeras from the imagination. We look along the
surface of society, and behold it illuminated by brilliant and beautiful lights; but if we venture to penetrate into its depths, we discover a whole universe of
errors, wild fancies, fables and fantastical creations,
springing up perpetually out of a bottomless gulf of
darkness. Comparatively few persons are entirely
free from these weaknesses. From the rulers of
mankind downwards, we find beliefs not founded in
reason, and irreconcileable with religion, flourishing
far and wide; faith in prodigies, in destiny, in astro-
logical fictions, in witchcraft, soothsaying, necromancy,
cheiromancy, and all the ridiculous paraphernalia of
barbarism.

The late trials and disclosures about witchcraft
have directed public attention to the amount of

superstition still existing in this country. Philosophers perhaps may upon the whole be free from it; but other men, even when gifted with the greatest genius, are often carried away by this original weakness of our nature. Thus Napoleon accepted one of the wildest doctrines of judicial astrology, imagining he had a star, which directed all his actions and determined their issues. His nephew also has his secret voice, his mission, his destiny, which place him on a level with the old women of the provinces. Here with us, men of the greatest distinction have given proof of being under the dominion of this superstition.

Lord Castlereagh used to tell a story of a Fire Spirit, which, at some great house in the country, once appeared to him in his bedroom.

It was a cold winter's night, and he had retired to bed, though not, as it appears, to sleep. He lay there musing, and looking at the embers of a large wood fire still smouldering on the hearth. At length he perceived a diminutive figure emerge from the flames, and advance towards his bed. At every step it increased in stature, until by the time it stood opposite him it had reached a gigantic height. What it said he never revealed, but having performed its mission, it retreated, diminishing as it went, until on reaching the hearth it plunged into the dying flames, and was lost to view.

There is a much older story of an English Earl, who sat deliberating in his mind whether or not he should join the expedition of the Pretender, then just landed in Scotland. His wife was with him at the time, although completely ignorant of his meditations. Suddenly she became convulsed with terror, and exclaimed, " O God, I see, I see it !" " What do you see ?" inquired her husband. " I see your head," she replied, " ghastly and dripping with blood, rolling across the floor towards your own feet." The Earl smiled, joined the expedition, and was beheaded.

Similar superstitions have existed all the world over. The suitors of Penelope foresee, in the Odyssey, their own death, which overtakes them exactly as their imagination represented it. These things, however, are not more remote from credibility than innumerable superstitions, great and small, which exist everywhere around us in our own day. In fact human nature reposes on a vast element of superstition, indestructible in its nature, which extends beneath our whole race, and moistens the very clay with which we are moulded.

In many parts of these islands, wild beliefs are so numerous that to describe them would require a

volume. A lady whom I knew, when her husband
was abroad, happened on a fine summer's evening
to be walking in fields dotted with fairy-rings. Her
thoughts of course were occupied with her absent
lord, when looking straight before her, over a stile,
she saw him distinctly by the moonlight coming along
the pathway towards her. She bounded forward,
mounted the stile, and was on the point of rushing
into his arms, when the figure vanished.

The same person returning home late at night,
through the unlighted streets of a country town, felt
herself suddenly in the midst of a crowd : the individuals of which it was composed moved noiselessly
along the pavement. She felt herself stifling. The
figures crept on at a funereal pace. Quickening her
steps, to escape from them, her forehead struck against
the corner of a coffin : upon this she shrieked aloud,
and in an instant the street was clear, the houses
and the solitary pavement appearing distinctly in
the starlight.

In the same part of the country, everybody believes
that nothing takes place in the material world which
is not represented previously in dumb show by
spirits. The figure of a ship which is to be wrecked,
and which at that moment may be a thousand miles
off on the Atlantic, appears at night upon the waves

with all its shrouds and canvass, its lights and its crew. It floats onwards, it mounts, it descends the surges, it dashes against the iron-bound coast, it goes to pieces; and then a multitude of small candles, each borne by a human figure, start from the water: they marshal themselves into a procession; they advance inward over the sand; they ascend the hills; they descend into the town; they traverse its midnight streets; they make their way towards the churchyard, where, one after another, they plunge into a new-made grave. Weeks or months afterwards the ship is wrecked, and the drowned sailors are buried in the very spot pointed out by the apparitions.

Again, on Allhallows Eve, an Angel, they say, takes its stand upon the chancel-table in the old church, and reads over in a loud voice the names of all the persons, big and little, who are to die during the following year. If any one overhears this terrible bead-roll, he is compelled to repair on Allhallows night for the remainder of his life, and there to stand on a tomb and listen to the Angel till his own name is called.

Sometimes these superstitions lead to mischief. In the western provinces of France it is believed, that a lantern made of an infant's skull renders him who bears it invisible. House-breakers therefore make themselves lanterns of this sort, and a man was executed a few winters ago for having murdered a child eleven months old, to obtain its skull for this purpose.

In many parts of England, where the fairies still maintain their ground, the milkmaids sprinkle water—the true descendant of holy water—about the dairy, to prevent the little people from dipping their whiskers in the milk-pans during the night. The same persons are also persuaded that witches often prefer to broomsticks fine handsome horses, and accordingly take them from the stable, and ride them over earth and water all night, though they are always very careful to bring them back before the morning. To prevent this, the grooms studiously stop up every aperture in wall and doors, by which a witch might be supposed to effect an entrance. Still the members of this sisterhood are so ingenious and powerful, that they get into the stables nevertheless, and ride the horses so furiously, that they are found in the morning trembling all over, and covered with sweat. It seems never to occur to the worthy grooms, that locking out the wholesome air may produce this effect.

The subject of witchcraft having been brought before the public, several persons have been induced to supply some curious illustrations of the manner in which the superstition works in many parts of the country. Some writers attribute the diffusion of the belief to the vitality of tradition, while others infer from that very vitality the existence of an occult law, which enables those individuals called witches to produce the effects ascribed to them.

It is said truly enough, that education cannot eradicate such opinions from the mind, because we cannot by education create in men faculties not bestowed on them by nature: we can only develope, elevate, and refine their understandings. Some persons, therefore, whatever they may be taught, will continue to cherish the belief in certain superstitions, witchcraft among the rest, to the end of their days.

Whenever this topic is discussed, people are sure to refer to Addison, who confessed that he believed in witchcraft; but this is no way surprising. Addison was not a philosopher, and did not possess that amount of intellect which renders a man independent of the notions of his age.

There are two movements in society: one which elevates the whole mass of the people, as volcanic action, upheaves an entire continent, and another which throws up the minds of some few individuals far above the intellectual level around them. Education represents the former, but the latter is occasioned by some unknown law, which gives to certain men a superiority over others. With this phenomenon civilization has nothing whatever to do. Zoroaster, Zaleucus, Lycurgus, Solon, Pythagoras, Socrates, were not wise because their neighbours were so. They derived their wisdom directly from Nature herself; their souls were not like those of other men. They produced great thoughts, and great deeds, by a necessity of their intellectual constitution, as a tree produces fruit.

But this fact by no means leads us to infer that education can do nothing for men. Everybody, in order to perform his duties in this world, must obtain it either through his own spontaneous energy, or through the ministry of others. In either case it is not always sure to deliver men from superstition, which is as much a disease of the mind as fever or small-pox is a disease of the body.

It has been thought that the seeds of all diseaess are in us always, though they require the breath of circumstances to call them into activity. It is admitted that we are born with the elements of all virtues and all vices, and may by certain influences be led to cultivate the one or the other, or both together. Superstition is a vice, and the well-spring of other vices. The belief in witchcraft, for example, hardens the heart, and leads to the persecution, and often to the murder, of the most helpless and innocent portion of our species. Society never appears in so despicable a light, as when it brings its irresistible power to bear against a poor, decrepit, harmless old woman, bowed down by poverty, want and sorrow.

We now discover, that here in England, in the midst of our civilization, with the light of Christianity, ready to pour into the meanest and darkest hovels, provided people will open their doors and windows to admit it,—in spite of our knowledge and religion,—I say, we discover a number of strong men throwing a ladder across a stream, dragging out an old woman, with one foot already in the grave, tying her petticoats about her feet, hurling her into the stream, and then trampling upon her furiously, because the inflation of her clothes would not let her sink. This practice of swimming witches has been in use from time immemorial, but was supposed to have died out with the eighteenth century, yet we find it still prevailing in our rural districts, while the belief in witches is all but universal.

I have said that superstition is indestructible, but its empire may be diminished by education. Persons of knowledge and experience do not in these days mistake mice, or flies, or spiders for so many imps of Satan, though we find farmers in our central counties not ashamed to acknowledge their own faith in such beliefs.

It is commonly imagined that superstition avoids great cities, and locates itself amid woods and streams in the depths of the country. A slight acquaintance with the inhabitants of London must speedily dissipate this idea. On the outskirts of our prodigious city, where the sheen of its gas-lamps mingles with the light of the glow-worm in the fields, beliefs as ancient as the world still prevail in unimpaired force. The Lamia of antiquity, that roamed about moonlit shores, and through the dark recesses of forests, to entrap and devour stray children, has found her way to the environs of London. In former times she was young and beautiful, but she has grown old with the world, and now appears in the shape of an aged though not decrepit woman, since she runs along nimbly in the dark, snatches up, and bears to the nearest pond any little urchin, male or female, whom she encounters on her way.

Two or three years ago there was a large sheet of water near the north-western suburbs, in which several children were drowned, through the agency, it was confidently believed, of a poor old woman who lived in a cottage close at hand. In consequence of her evil reputation, the juveniles persecuted her so vigorously, that she was constrained to leave the neighbourhood. Had she lived in Ireland, or in the central counties of England, she would have been swum for a witch, and perhaps drowned in the very pond in which her supposed victims had perished.

Another form of superstition is putting faith in dreams. All the world over, men have perplexed themselves by endeavouring to extract a prophetic meaning from the fantastic creations of sleep. The best cure for such weakness is to pay no attention to this brood of night. Persons of active minds seldom do, because in the real waking world they find sufficient employment for their thoughts. The weak, or those who are rendered indolent by disease, often pay attention to the images that disturb their fancies at night. If they would give themselves the trouble to study the philosophy of the subject, they would find that the character of our dreams depends almost entirely on the condition of our bodies. Persons who have been accustomed in childhood to run to their mothers at the slightest touch of ill-health, will be apt to dream of their mothers as often as they are unwell during the remainder of their lives.

I have myself, under the influence of fever, in the deserts of Africa, dreamed nightly of my childhood's home. As soon as my eyes closed, I was borne back

through years and distance to the beautiful garden
in which I had played when a child.   The box-edged
borders, the beehives, the sweet flowers, the blossom-
ing shrubs, were all around me; and the power of
sleep threw open the grave, and brought forth my
mother, in all her beauty and tenderness, to soothe
me as of old.   I have known persons who, when
happy, always dreamed of the sea-shore, over which
they wandered in the delicious sunshine of childhood, picking up rare shells, and running backwards
and forwards after the tiny waves.

Had dreams been intended to pre-signify the future,
they would certainly have been differently moulded.
As it is, their use seems to be, to soothe and amuse
us in health by delighting our imaginations, and to
warn us when we transgress the laws of temperance.
They are often the mere children of diet.   Dryden used
to eat raw pork for supper, in order to feast his imagination on hideous dreams; and if people were to study
at once their diet and their dreams, they would find
that one was little more than a consequence of the
other.

The sleep of those who live in cities is peopled with
images very different from such as revel in the dream-
life of a savage, or of one who wanders in forests and
deserts.   Persons of a poetical and spiritual tempera-

ment dream of God, of heaven, of angels, of aspiring mountains, of clouds, of vast rivers, of the ocean; while the sleep of material individuals is conversant with ideas little more elevated than those which constitute the staple of their ordinary thoughts.

It seems to follow from this view of the matter that nothing can be more irrational than oneiromancy, or the art of foretelling the future by dreams. It is a mere superstition, which, as I said before, is a vice, because it weakens the mental powers, and withdraws them from their legitimate occupation, which is to accumulate the materials of happiness both for the individual and the community.

CHAPTER IV.

OUR OWN HISTORY AND INSTITUTIONS.

Our own History and Institutions.—What the People are expected
to read.—Study of Home Things.—Position of the English as
a People.—They resemble no other Nation.—The Englishman
abroad.—Reason why he is disliked.—The first step towards
a true Education.—Want of a National History.—Wrong system of Instruction.—Our Energies exhausted in external Researches.—Classical History and Literature.—False Ideas of
vulgarity.—Scholars and Travellers.—Anecdote of a Scottish
Earl.—Roman Policy and Grecian Genius.—Power and Grandeur
of England.—Contrast between Great Britain and Rome.—Heroic
Period of our History.—Dominions of England in every division
of the World.—Highest Pinnacle of the Earth.—The numerous
Races under British Rule.—Our Parliament and Armies.—Our
Dominion the Dominion of Intellect.—Knowledge of the Growth
and Structure of our Empire rare.—The English Church.—
Catholic Priests.—Dissenting Ministers.—Universities, Colleges,
Schools.—Ignorance of God.—No Church for the Poor.—Oriental
Mosques.—The Mission of the Pulpit.—Diffusion of Christianity.—
Religious and Secular Instruction.

IT would be extremely difficult to say what, up to
this hour, we have aimed at. Perhaps the education
of the working classes is imperfect, chiefly because

that of the superior classes is so.   The national mind appears to be very much in the dark on the subject of teaching and learning.   We talk of the classics and the sciences, of poetry and fiction, of knowledge useful and knowledge ornamental, and then undertake to decide for the people what they ought or ought not to read.

Do we ourselves however know what we ought to read?   And if we do, do we read what we ought? As Englishmen our first aim should be to comprehend what is the signification of the term England in the existing state of things.   Knowledge, like charity, should begin at home.   Men's energies should obviously move at first in the narrowest possible circle : they should try to know a little of themselves, a little of their neighbours, a little of their country, and then, by degrees, a little of the rest of the world.

As a people we occupy a very remarkable position among civilized communities.   Our geographical situation is peculiar, I might almost say unique; our institutions range under the same category; we resemble no other people in our language, in our literature, in our philosophy, or even in our religion.   All these things have been modified among us by the national character, which is profoundly stamped on every idea that emanates from the mind of every one

of our countrymen,—a truth which we commonly
express by saying that this or that notion is or is not
English. This in our mouths is not an unmeaning
phrase, but points out emphatically the differences
existing between us and the other nations of Christendom.

When an Englishman goes abroad, he is seldom
mistaken for the inhabitant of any other country : he
has an obvious stamp on him, by which he is known
everywhere. It is not in his countenance, in his
gait, in his bearing, still less in his dress; it is in
the whole man. There is about him an air of independence, of superiority, of command, which generally
renders him disagreeable. People dislike him without
exactly knowing why; but the reason is that he hu-
miliates them by bringing up forcibly before their
minds their own enslaved and half-menial condition,
while his air proves unmistakably that he is his own
master, and profoundly conscious of it.

Well, the first thing a boy or youth in England
should be taught is the cause of the national idiosyn-
crasy of which I have been speaking. Why are we
different from the rest of the world ? Let us begin
our education by understanding that; and how is this
knowledge to be acquired ? It is natural, of course,
to reply, by studying the history of our own country.

But what history? Who has cast our annals into the form calculated at once to rivet the attention of the people, and to enlighten their minds respecting their origin, the rise and progress of their language, of their literature, of their institutions, of their religion? I know of no such history.

As things stand at present, the most learned and indefatigable Englishman can hardly, by the time he has reached middle life, be said to comprehend thoroughly the growth, moral, intellectual, political, and religious, of the nation to which he belongs. We are only now, at this eleventh hour of our existence, beginning with anything like perseverance and system to study ourselves. Hitherto our curiosity has busied itself chiefly with remote times and regions. We have mapped out the world of study after an extraordinary fashion, and, commencing at the periphery, have endeavoured, with much pains and labour, to make our way towards the centre, which should have formed our starting-point.

By this I may seem to be condemning all investigations into classical antiquity, all acquaintance with the great empires which flourished during remote ages in central and western Asia, in the valley of the Nile, in Hellas, and in Italy; all attempts at enlarging and enlightening our minds, by familiarizing them

with what was done in old times in philosophy, in
literature, in political eloquence, and in the science of
government; by taking a vast survey of those obscure
and tumultuous movements by which the human race
sought, in the early stages of its existence, to get into
the true track of civilization, and thus, through immense energy and suffering, laid the foundation of
that social happiness which we now enjoy.

Such however is not my intention. I only maintain that when, through the force of circumstances,
the choice is imposed upon us whether we will remain ignorant of ourselves, and of our own country and
history, or of other nations whose cycle of existence
has been long closed, we should prefer what comes
home nearest to our own business and bosoms. Here
in England has our lot been cast, and therefore with
the things which relate to England ought we to become first acquainted : and yet how few of the wisest
and most prudent among us pursue this course !

Until very recently something like an idea of vulgarity attached to the study of home geography, home
antiquities, and home history. To be a scholar, was
to be acquainted exclusively with Greek and Latin ;
while to be a traveller, was to go abroad to visit foreign
courts, to scale the Alps, to dive into mummy-pits, or
to wander among half-naked savages over the plains

of Africa or Asia. In illustration of this truth an amusing anecdote is related of a Scotch nobleman. Happening one day to be conversing in northern Italy with a travelled lover of the picturesque, he was surprised to hear him mention, among the most beautiful cascades in the world, a waterfall in Scotland. "In what part of Scotland?" inquired the North Briton. His companion explained. "Bless me!" exclaimed our countryman, "that is on my own estate, though I never heard of it till now; I will go back, however, and see it before I prosecute my foreign travels any further." He was a sensible man; and it would be creditable to us all were we to go and do likewise.

If we would have the people look at home, we should be at the pains to allure them into the study of England, and everything that relates to it. But this is not to be accomplished by cant and misrepresentation. It is not true, as some have maintained, that our literature is the finest in the world: and still less is it true that our empire, politically and socially speaking, is the greatest that has ever existed. We are as yet very far from having reached that predominance among mankind which belonged to the ancient Romans; very far from having exhibited that prolific power of creation which once distinguished the Greek race in literature, philosophy, and art.

What then? Are we on this account to conclude that the growth of our empire is undeserving of profound study; or that our poets, our orators, our philosophers, our historians, are not capable of imparting to the diligent student instruction, wisdom, and delight? Far from it. The rise and spread of the English power have developed social and political phenomena, characterized by greater grandeur, and fraught with more fertile instruction, than those which mark the fortunes of any other modern people. The growth of our empire exhibits a striking contrast to that of Rome. The Republic of the Seven Hills, springing from small beginnings, consolidated itself gradually, conquered and incorporated one small state after another, overpassed the Alps, the Adriatic, the Mediterranean; and, still surging outwards in one compact body, covered the whole civilized world with its shields, and roused it into activity by the tramp of its legions. Wherever its eagles flew, there was victory; wherever it placed its foot, arts and civilization appeared. Its colonies implanted the seeds of refinement in the East and in the West; and whatever progress modern nations have made towards enlightenment, they owe more or less directly to the Roman commonwealth.

England has been compelled by the laws of her

existence to pursue a totally different course. In the heroic ages of our monarchy the princes of the country precipitated vast armies upon the Continent, gained brilliant victories, and achieved numerous conquests, but in the course of a very short time nothing remained to the victors but the fame of their exploits. Driven back to their own island, they happily applied themselves to the achievement of victories over nature, and, by cultivating the soil and exploring the vast circumference of the ocean, commenced that mighty and glorious career which we are still pursuing.

Nevertheless, our empire is anything but homogeneous and compact. It lies scattered here and there over the whole surface of the globe, from the Arctic to the Antarctic, and comprises regions covered with perpetual snow, and others which glow eternally under the direct rays of the Equator.

Rome, when its dominions were most widely diffused, never comprehended within its limits tracts so utterly dissimilar to each other. In the British territories rises the loftiest pinnacle of the earth, forming part of a range of mountains to which the Alps are pigmies. Among our fellow-citizens are men of almost every variety, in language, colour, and creed, belonging to every stage of civilization, from that which verges upon the highest refinement hitherto known, down to the dusky savage, who sleeps at night under a basket, or wanders naked and houseless over the barren and desolate plains of Australasia.

This mighty dominion, so diversified in aspect, so strangely peopled, obeys laws made during the winter months at a house in Westminster. Yes, upwards of two hundred and forty millions of human beings, that is, more than a fifth of the whole human race, have the conditions of their existence regulated by the deliberations of a handful of Englishmen. And how is this brought about? We are far from possessing the largest armies in the world. We do not, in fact, develope our power in the military form. How then do we rule that immense portion of the earth which has fallen to our share? By the force of intelligence, by the very thing which it is the object of the present age to diffuse universally among the people,—I mean, education.

" Knowledge," observes Bacon, " is power ;" and none of the phenomena of history, from the days of Ninus to the days of Lord Palmerston, ever more strikingly illustrated this truth than the spread of the British empire. It ought, consequently, to form one of the pleasures of Englishmen and English-women to learn how this wonderful structure sprang up and developed itself. Yet the idea of imparting

such knowledge to high or low does not appear to
have suggested itself to the minds of our teachers.
At all events, it is by no means common to meet
with persons in any rank of life who understand very
distinctly of what elements the British dominions
consist, how many they are, where they lie, and by
what sort of inhabitants they are peopled. This
knowledge, of course, is by no means a *sine quâ
non.* I only contend that it is pleasant to possess
it, pleasant to acquire it, and no less pleasant, under
certain conditions, to impart it.

When we speak of the education of the people, we
generally confine our views to the inhabitants of
these islands, and make no reference to the Hin-
doos, or Mohammedans, Malays, New Zealanders, Aus-
tralians, Caffres, or Hottentots. We think, and think
correctly, that we have just now enough to do at home.

At the first view, we appear to possess a sufficient
apparatus for imparting knowledge to the population.
We have a church more richly endowed than any in
the world, and commanding the services of fifteen or
twenty thousand ministers, whose exclusive business
it is to instruct the people in religion. We have a
Catholic hierarchy in one part of the empire; we
have a prodigious number of dissenting ministers
diffused all over the country; we have ancient and

wealthy universities, colleges, academies, schools without number; and yet a majority of the humbler classes are either altogether without knowledge, or but very imperfectly instructed.

When individuals are taken up and brought to justice for any offence against the law, they frequently prove to be wholly ignorant of the first rudiments of religion. They scarcely know what is meant by the word God; they have no notion, save that which comes by instinct, of immortality; they have not been taught to comprehend, even in the humblest way, the doctrine of human responsibility; they have never been taught to pray, and, if they possess any ideas of morality, they must have acquired them by mere accident.

Obviously this is not a desirable state of things. It is of no use to pretend, as some do, that there is a church open for all, and that they may go thither every Sunday and be instructed. There is no church open for all. Nearly the whole area of our sacred edifices is covered with warmly-closed, well-cushioned, and well-hassocked pews, in which the wealthy may worship God at their ease. For the poor there is nothing left but long draughty passages, where, on hard benches, they may sit apart, exposed to colds rheumatisms, coughs, and consumptions, and scorn-

fully looked down upon by the opulent. The House
of God should be free to all; and all should, there at
least, be treated in the same manner. If you go into
a Mohammedan mosque, you behold the Pasha and
the peasant standing or kneeling side by side, without the slightest distinction. Neither money, nor the
power of money, exhibits its influence there. All
enter unimpeded, all stand or sit where they please.
There are no reserved seats in the presence of the
Almighty, and people learn there the great lesson
that there is one spot at least in this world, where
men are invested with the original rights of their
nature, and stand equal before their Maker.

When they go forth again into the world, they
resume their ranks and distinctions, their titles and
their privileges ; but the poor always remember with
a secret joy that religion recognizes no differences
among men, but those which spring from greater or
less degrees of piety and virtue.

It would be well then if in this respect we were
to imitate the children of the Muslims. No harm
could possibly arise to us from a practice which the
Mohammedans themselves borrowed from the early
Christians, and which might now return to us from
our forefathers, through the intermediation of the
professors of El Islam.

But supposing the people in church, and well contented with their situation, is it possible that the very ignorant can profit greatly by what they hear? The Latin of the Mass-book is almost as intelligible to Roman Catholic congregations as the sermons of our clergy to the poor. The fault, however, is not always, nay, not often, in them. They could not, by any contrivance, preach down to the level of the un-instructed. The mind must be prepared from infancy before it can take in knowledge rapidly, as it is delivered from the pulpit, and frequently, after all, even the educated derive small profit from what they hear in half an hour at church.

To render the clergy equal to their duties, they themselves ought to undergo a different system of training and instruction. Christianity is now an old religion, having been preached to the world for nearly two thousand years; but it has been always growing, and is increasing still. Nevertheless, it must be obvious to the most careless observer, that it might be made to diffuse its blessings yet more rapidly and widely.

Christ's ministry in Palestine lasted but three years, yet at the period of his death there were very few persons within the limits of the land who had not seen or heard him preach. His divine voice appeared to vibrate through the whole atmosphere. He passed from place to place. He was beheld everywhere. The rich might listen if they pleased, but his Gospel was preached chiefly to the poor. Why ? Because, if you purify and ennoble the foundations of society, the remainder will take care of itself. The Church of Christ should not be above doing now what he himself did then. What we want is, not a multitude of new structures, but the appearance of a new spirit among us, the spirit of goodwill to all. We should regard it as a reproach to us as a nation, that any man or woman among us is suffered to grow up to years of discretion without being instructed in those truths which form the basis of our social system.

I am not, however, one of those who think the education of the people should consist entirely of religious teaching. They ought not to be left in ignorance of their religion, but should at the same time be allured into the acquisition of other kinds of knowledge. The prejudiced and the narrow-minded would give them nothing but the Scriptures, or tracts, or sermons. But will they read them ?—That is the question. If they won't, what will they read ? I answer, precisely the same books that are read by other persons,—poetry, novels, biography, light and lively books of travels, and history sometimes, when it is well written.

The *Times*, speaking of the education of the people, observes, with as much vivacity as truth : " What reasonable excuse can be assigned for the distinction, that the mass of the population are to be brought up exclusively religious, and the better classes almost exclusively profane? Why are workmen, labourers, and maid-servants to be merely theologians, and their masters only scholars and *savants ?* Of course the attempt does not answer ; but even if it did, why should it ever be made ? We set small value by the Graces and the Muses, when we so carefully deny the sight of them to our peasantry, and to all the sons and daughters of toil."

The attempt to make the people exclusively religious has everywhere failed, because it is opposed to all the laws that regulate human nature. All we can reasonably desire is, that our literature, whether designed for the benefit of high or low, should be pervaded by a religious spirit, which need not interfere with the amusement or pleasure it may be calculated to afford. Shakespeare is at once the most amusing and the most religious of poets. When treating of affairs merely of this world he keeps his vast imagination in check, and allows it to place before

the mind none but images of recreation and vivacity. He excites merriment, he provokes laughter,
he throws a warm and joyous colouring over the
fancy; but when he has done this, he does not
consider that he has done all. From time to time,
at intervals chosen with exquisite art, he opens up
before the mind a prospect into another world, and
brings down ideas from a higher sphere, to chasten
and correct the impulses of sense and the promptings of ordinary ambition. Who, accordingly, can read
'Hamlet' or 'Macbeth' or 'Lear,' without being
impressed with awe and veneration for that mighty
agency by which the whole universe is governed?

CHAPTER V.

POETS, NOVELISTS, NEWSPAPERS.

Chaucer.—Neglect of our Poets.—Spenser.—Marlowe and the other Dramatists.—Milton.—Shakspeare.—Dryden.—Pope.—The Modern Poets.—Opinion of Charles James Fox.—Poets not immoral. —The writings of the Prophets.—Poetry the earliest form of instruction.—Figurative Language of Barbarians.—Prose less natural than Poetry.—Novels and Romances.—Novels hostile to the Drama. —Excellence of the Epic.—Sources of its power over the Heart. —Last parting of Husband and Wife.—A Father begging the Body of his Son.—Fictions in Prose.—Corrupt Authors in corrupt times.—Manly Character of our Literature.—Newspapers.—Their Influence in Educating the People.—Pages in the History of the World.

It happens fortunately that the literature of England abounds more than that of any other country in poetry,—and poetry, moreover, of the very highest order. Here is a vast field of delight thrown open to the very humblest of our countrymen, for it is one characteristic of poetry, that it is at once more fascinating and intelligible than prose. Lord Palmerston, speaking on this subject, puts forward much the same opinion. " Why," he asks, " should not a day of fatigue be relieved in the evening by the occasional indulgence in the pleasure of poetry, and in that delightful enjoyment which the best works of fiction impart? Such occasional recreations, though they ought not to be the sole object of reading, are nevertheless useful, by giving buoyancy to the intellect, and inspiring the mind with noble sentiments and feelings which deserve to be cultivated."

Were it not for the obsoleteness of his language, which repels people at first, the oldest of our poets would also be the most popular.* Chaucer is thoroughly and intensely English. He does not appear so much to speak the sentiments of one man, as to embody the feelings, passions, and ideas of a whole generation. England is above all things merry England in Chaucer. Without being, properly speaking, comic, he is full of mirth, humour, and vivacity. He paints every class among his contemporaries, from the polished and love-sick knight, dreaming of his mistress in forests and castles, down to the jolly monk and tavern host, chirping and singing over their cups.

---

* The French people, who in general know so little of our literature, may now familiarize themselves with the principal work of Chaucer through M. de Chatelain's translation of " The Canterbury Tales," the result of a long and diligent study of our antique bard.

In the works of no one man are the elements of amusement more thickly sown. His variety is prodigious. He looked abroad as far as his knowledge would permit, and with a bold hand seized upon the literary wealth of all Christendom and transplanted it ingeniously into his mother-tongue. Of course he is tiresome occasionally, because he endeavours to expound in his verses the theories of religion, morals, criticism, and love, of which he had rendered himself master. But perhaps his contemporaries never thought him tedious. At any rate, if a man wishes to understand the character of our forefathers, their morals, manners, loves, friendships, the degree of freedom they enjoyed, the store of home delights and amusements at their command, their intelligence, their liveliness, their humour, their moral tastes, their estimable and manly temper of mind, he must become, by hook or by crook, acquainted with Chaucer.

Though the educated classes of this country are much given to reading and study, we yet neglect most egregiously the poetical riches we possess. If any other nation in Europe could boast of poets like ours, they would not only erect statues to them, but convert their works, reprinted by millions, into monuments infinitely grander and more enduring. There is Spenser, for example, with his ' Faery Queen ;' in what literature do we meet with a series of softer, more fanciful, or brilliant landscapes? One fault Spenser undoubtedly has,—in fact, he has many faults,—but the one I am about to speak of is the chief of them. He affected the use of antiquated words. He looked upon Chaucer as " a well of English undefiled," and, through admiration, not only reproduced his obsolete language, but borrowed crabbed and unmusical terms from other writers, or else invented them himself. This drawback, however, is not great; a very slight degree of perseverance will enable any one to master the difficulties of Spenser.

Marlowe, a far greater genius, clothes his ideas in the most transparent English. Ben Jonson, Beaumont and Fletcher, Decker and Webster, Middleton, Massinger, and Ford, are seldom obscure, though objections may sometimes perhaps be raised against the nature of their subjects, and even against the titles of their plays.

It would not be a little superfluous to dwell upon the merits of Milton and Shakespeare, two of the greatest names in the whole literature of the world. In the former we possess the superior of all modern epic poets, and in the latter the greatest and most original genius, with one single exception, that ever applied itself to poetry in any age or country.

We must not, however, take it for granted, on account of the transcendent merits of Shakespeare and Milton, that their writings are familiar to a majority of the English people, though the circle of their popularity is widening daily. It requires no small degree of education to be able to deal with the great thoughts of Shakespeare, or with the high and sublime language in which they are habitually clothed. The reading of other poets, less, but not therefore little, may serve to prepare the mind for the study of Milton and Shakespeare, the highest and noblest enjoyment which literature can afford. Dryden, Pope, Gray, Cowper, Wordsworth, Coleridge, Byron, Keats, Scott, Shelley, with numbers among our own contemporaries, deserve to be in the hands of the people, not only for the purpose of enlarging their minds, but to soothe them after their labours, and give them a true relish of existence. Charles James Fox, who loved everything that was great and beautiful, set a pre-eminent value on the works of the poets. Addressing himself to those who aim in any way at distinguishing themselves, he says, " I am of opinion that the study of good authors, and especially poets, ought never to be intermitted by any man who is to speak or write for the public, or indeed who has any occasion to tax his imagination, whether it be for argument, for illustration, for ornament, for sentiment, or for any other purpose."

Many persons, I am aware, anathematize the poets as teachers of immorality; but this is absurd. No poet ever set himself about teaching immorality. He may have written things which strict morality would condemn, but the sum of his ideas taken together would, nevertheless, be found to improve as well as to delight the mind. In the earlier stages of society poets are often somewhat coarse, but cheerful, buoyant, and calculated to inspire contentment. In later periods they are more polished, refined, and fastidious in their language, but at the same time gloomier, more morbid, discontented, and depressing.

I dwell on this subject because it is the most closely connected with that of religion. The Prophets were poets also; and if their works were detached from the general body of the Scriptures, and printed separately with explanatory introductions, Isaiah, Joel, Habakkuk, Ezekiel, would inevitably find their way, through the mere beauty of their ideas, into every cottage in the empire. I would studiously avoid everything like expounding or commentary, and leave the glorious compositions to make their way through the force of their own excellence. When they have been left fairly to themselves they never have failed yet; and it may be safely affirmed that they never will fail to exalt, ennoble, and purify the soul which is familiarized with them.

All nations at the outset of their career have made use of poetry to instruct the great body of the people. Truth, beautiful in all places, is yet rendered more beautiful when robed with metaphor and simile, adorned with all kinds of fresh and glittering imagery, and infused into the mind through the channel of harmonious verse. The maxims of wisdom, Divine or human, are never so easily treasured up in the memory as when they have been moulded by the poet's hand. They then easily find a place in the mind, and appear to be always ready winged to fly forth on every fitting occasion.

All philosophers have observed that nations and tribes of men advanced very little beyond the state of nature are always remarkable for the poetical character of their language; and the uneducated classes throughout the world are necessarily in almost the same condition with those tribes and nations. When any individual from among them, therefore, rises above the level of ignorance, and grasps at the skirts of literature, it is the golden fringes of poetry that he first lays hold of. Strange as it may seem, prose, in its more elevated forms, is much further removed

from nature than poetry, and is consequently more
completely out of the reach of undisciplined and
uneducated minds.   When the breath of inspiration
passes over them, they do not construct syllogisms,
or meddle with the infinitely raised figures of rhetoric,
but literally lisp in numbers.

This fact alone should suffice to convince us that
the proper method of impregnating the popular mind
with knowledge is to begin with the poets.

Next after these in order come the authors of novels
and romances. I am perfectly aware that there exists
a widely-spread prejudice against this class of compositions.   But what is a novel?   Is it not a picture
of life, more or less skilfully drawn, according to the
genius and intelligence of the writer ?   I once knew
a lady highly educated, travelled, and gifted besides
with intellectual faculties of no common order, who
having fallen into ill-health, used to say that she
possessed no means of acquainting herself with the
movements of society but the novels of the day.   To
her they supplied at once the place of conversation
and experience.

Whether the result be fortunate or otherwise, novels
have gone a great way towards extinguishing the
drama in this country. People can now, by their
own firesides, delight their imaginations with more

surprising turns of fortune than they can possibly witness on the stage. The play-writer has much fewer materials at his command than the novelist. The latter can take a vaster scope, introduce a greater number of characters, present more multiplied incidents, and enter more minutely into details. Every well-constructed novel is a sort of humble epic. It does not indeed deal with the destinies of empires, but it deals separately with those destinies—the destinies of families,—which, taken together, make up the destinies of the mightiest states. In proportion, too, as they descend from generalities to particulars, from wars, battles, sieges, to the struggles and sufferings of individuals, to blighted and ruined hearths, or to the rising of men from small beginnings to distinction through the exercise of energy and virtue,—in proportion as they do this, I say, they possess a profounder interest, and exercise a more irresistible power over the mind.

I would not however be understood to maintain that the novel, such as we possess it, is equal in excellence to the epic. The latter brings into play feelings and sentiments nobler, because farther removed from self; yet what are the passages in the greatest poems which touch the deepest sources of sympathy in our nature? Are they not the parting of husband and wife, of friend and friend, of parents and children ? When we have beheld with comparative calmness the mowing down of whole squadrons in the field, is not our heart overwhelmed suddenly with tenderness by beholding an old man, bent down by the weight of years and sorrow, prostrating himself before an enemy in the dust, to beg from him for interment the body of a beloved son ? Here the epic becomes confounded with the domestic interest, and the king does not sink, but rise, into the father.

Our own history supplies an incident in some points parallel with this. After the battle of Hastings, when the mother of the dauntless Harold came to beg of the Norman Duke the body of her son, as remarkable for manly beauty as any chief celebrated in poetry, she met from the conqueror a stern refusal. Not however discouraged, she still pressed her suit, and having urged in vain all the motives supplied by maternal tenderness, concluded by appealing to his avarice, and offered the body's weight in gold.

Some of our historians, influenced by a sense of poetical fitness, represent William as yielding to the mother's eloquence and refusing the corpse's ransom ; but the chroniclers of most credit relate that he persisted in his unfeeling policy, and ordered the remains of his rival to be interred with indignity on that shore, says the chronicler, which it had been so long his glory to defend.

It will not, I trust, be maintained by any that Homer, Virgil, and Milton, with their glorious fictions, have the slightest tendency to corrupt the mind; and if they have not, why should we attribute any such tendency to the writers of fictions in prose? No doubt when states verge towards their decline, the corruption of society appears to engender authors who labour to facilitate that corruption, and hasten the degeneracy of manners, but our literature at present exhibits no such features. Instead of sinking from bad to worse, it is assuming constantly a more healthful and manly tone.

There is another class of works which many, I fear, would be sorry to recommend to the people, and yet it exercises a far greater influence than all the other departments of literature put together,—I mean, the newspapers. It is one of the effects of a state of civilization like that at which we have arrived, to render us so familiar with great advantages, as to blind us altogether to their value. This is pre-eminently the case with the newspaper. How few of us consider what it is! We read it frequently without being conscious that it is a page in the history of the world, and that, if we reflect upon it maturely, it will do for us what no other history, however ably written, can possibly achieve. It lays open to us every portion of the mighty fabric of society, the deliberations of senates, the movements of armies, the operations of commerce and industry, the growth of laws and institutions, the contests of wealth and poverty, and the most fearful excesses of crime. This task is performed with more or less integrity and ability, by numerous journals in various parts of the empire, daily and weekly, and we cannot possibly understand the state of that society in which we live, without studying assiduously the fugitive historians of the hour.

CHAPTER VI.

PHYSICAL SCIENCES, IDEA OF GOD, SELF-INSTRUCTION.

Stupendous Mechanism of the Universe.—Interest of Astronomy.—
Its beneficial effect upon the mind.—How far accessible to the
Working Classes.—Defence of Smattering.—Infinite Varieties of
Knowledge.—Metaphysics.—Lord Stanley, Pope, and Lord Bacon.
—Birth of Scepticism.—Its Cure.—Well-spring of real Greatness.—
Simplicity of Religion.—Genesis of Morals.—Acquisition of Know-
ledge.—Our first Duty.—Self-taught Men.—Paradox of Helvetius.
—Development of Mental Power.—The Force of Opportunity.—
Different Capacities of Men.—Self-Discipline.—The Home of Ideas.
—Supremacy of Genius.—Shakespeare, Jean-Jacques, Burns, and
Chatterton.—Educational Tax.—" The Times."

THERE is a strong tendency at present to give a
preference over most other studies to the physical
sciences. Lord Stanley, a man of high intellect and
earnest character, in a speech of much power and
originality, recommended the mechanics of Oldham
to pursue this course; others, with equal earnestness,
but much inferior eloquence, have put forward the
same views. It is no doubt true that astronomy, for

example, throws open to us the most wonderful of all prospects, that of the universe, extending in stupendous grandeur immeasurably away into the abysses of space. By profound study and application, the genius of man has discovered many of the laws by which the movements of the universe are regulated. But darkness still hangs, and must for ever hang, over its interior mechanism, as well as over all the causes which generate motion, life, light, attraction, gravitation, and so on.

We observe the phenomena, and discover that this or that cause constantly produces such and such effects; but how or why it produces them, is still as much an enigma as it was when Prometheus hung suspended against the cliffs of Mount Caucasus. But to look out at night upon the stars and planets, and to observe through a large telescope the structure and infinitely varied motions of the mighty creation around us, cannot fail to call forth the power and awaken the curiosity of the mind. From the contemplation of such objects, a man returns to his daily avocations with increased respect for himself and other men, and with a stronger disposition to adore the All-powerful Maker of what he has beheld.

It would, however, as Lord Palmerston has observed, be highly unreasonable to expect a working man to become an astronomer, a geometrician, or a geologist; some insight he may, doubtless, acquire into various sciences, if, when the vast map of knowledge is unrolled before him, these departments of investigation happen to inspire him with more delight than any others. Nevertheless he must, as a rule, remain content with accepting the result of other men's researches and calculations; that is, must take information on trust, since he would find it impracticable to go through all those processes by which demonstration is attained.

Profoundly learned men, not gifted with the indulgent spirit of philosophy, may call persons thus instructed, smatterers;* but the aim of popular teaching is rather to create the appetite for knowledge than to supply all that is wanted. " Half a loaf," says the proverb, " is better than no bread." The

---

* Lord Palmerston's remarks on this subject are so just, that I shall introduce them here :—" A little knowledge is better than no knowledge at all. The more knowledge a man has, the better; but if his time and the means at his disposal do not permit of his acquiring deep and accurate knowledge, let him have as much as he can, and depend upon it he will be all the better for it. And although he may not be able to drink deeply of that spring, if his lips have once tasted of it, he will go back to the same delicious waters whenever he has an opportunity, and his draughts, be they great or small, will refresh his fancy, invigorate his intellect, raise him in the scale of civilization, contribute to his individual happiness, and make him a more useful and honourable member of society."

fact that we can't know all that we wish, is no reason
why we should not know all we can. To be a smat-
terer, therefore, is better than to be ignorant. The
world of knowledge is immense, so that no mind,
however powerful, can grasp it all. We must divide
map, and parcel it out into departments more or less
minute, so that every man, according to the bent of
his genius, may enter the field and set up his intellectual tabernacle on the spot which appears most
pleasant to his mind.

The great object is to allure all men to take up
their sickles and help to bring in the universal
harvest. Every sheaf need not be of the same grain,
or of the same dimensions; but its possessor, whatever it may be, will feel, as he bears it to the garner
of his mind, the delight of having been usefully employed. In this process there should be no mimicking,
and no dictation. Whatever Nature inclines a man
to prefer, she, at the same time, qualifies him to excel
in, if he is to excel in anything. Repugnance, properly understood, means inaptitude, while preference
signifies the reverse.

As there are many different kinds of work to be
done in the world, the wisdom of nature has provided
that there shall be men with all kinds of predilections and qualifications. There are individuals, for

example, who love to wander through the labyrinth
of metaphysics, and experience supreme pleasure in
watching those dim and equivocal lights which break
upon its tortuous avenues from on high; there they
could for ever remain engaged in the pursuit of
ideas and theories more or less sublime, and systems
which elevate and aggrandise the soul. Others, again,
with totally different aptitudes, glide by the force of
natural propensities into the study of the physical
sciences; they love what has length, and breadth, and
palpable dimensions.

Lord Stanley quotes, on the subject of smattering,
Pope's well-known lines,

> " A little learning is a dangerous thing ;
> Drink deep, or taste not the Pierian spring :
> There shallow draughts intoxicate the brain,
> But drinking largely sobers us again."

This is merely stating in verse what Lord Bacon
had previously said in prose—" A little learning doth
incline men to atheism, but proficiency in learning
bringeth him back again to religion." It is therefore
in reference to religion only, that a little learning is
here supposed to be dangerous.

Accordingly, we often find that men who have just
entered on the study of philosophy undergo a complete unsettling of all their ordinary notions. Seeing

that they have believed many things which they now discover to be wrong, they jump to the conclusion that all they have believed must be wrong.

It gratifies their conceit and vanity, to look, in matters of faith, over the heads of their neighbours, to inflate themselves with ideas of their own wisdom, and, turning their backs upon the rising sun, to admire the length of their own shadows, judging by which, they imagine themselves to be giants. But as the sun of knowledge rises, their shadows diminish, until, at high noon, they almost look for them in vain upon the ground. It is at this point in a man's studies that philosophy hands him over to religion. Having discovered his own littleness, he is glad to be led to something great, and admits with inexpressible joy the idea of God into his soul. This dilating gives him the consciousness of true greatness, and he begins to feel his real strength when he learns to lean upon his Maker.

It is the simplicity of religion that, to certain minds, renders it unattractive. They look for something involved, intricate, obscure, mysterious; but all great things come to us arrayed in simplicity. Nothing is more simple or natural than that created things should show obedience to their Creator; that they who have received much should love much, and that on this love they should base worship.

From the worship of God spring all the laws of morality, by a process of reasoning as simple as the common rules of arithmetic. If God be our Father, mankind are our brethren; and it is the obvious duty of brothers to love and aid each other. Again, brothers, by nature, receive equal portions from their father, which forms the basis of the law of property; but when some waste and others save, Justice steps in, and shows that good conduct and bad conduct must be suffered to produce their natural consequences; that the idle and profligate shall be punished by privation, and the virtuous and industrious rewarded by plenty.

Then comes the question of knowledge, and why it is useful. To perform our duties towards God or man, we must obviously know in what they consist and how we are to perform them. Hence the acquisition of knowledge comes to be placed at the head of our duties. By pursuing this course, we might show how every act of our lives has reference, directly or indirectly, to the idea of God, which is consequently the foundation, not only of religion, but of all politics and morality. Politics, in fact, are only the morals of a state, while morals are the politics of an individual, since they mean nothing more than the bundle of rules by which a man or a community should regulate his or its proceedings.

Considerations like these may perhaps reconcile us to the trifling exhibitions of vanity which we witness in self-taught men at the commencement of their studies. The mind loves to create and build up, because such acts are accompanied by a sense of power. We should not, however, infer that among the millions whom a national system of education must influence, there will be any great number of persons disposed to carry the development of their minds very far.

It was a paradox of Helvetius, that all men are by nature equal, and owe the differences which appear in them entirely to education. Though this be not true, it is true that the powers of all men are much greater than they suppose. Yet even this may appear to be a paradox, because, if it be said that we do not acquire knowledge, or exhibit intellectual force, because we want industry, the obvious answer is, that the absence of industry is weakness, and that we would use the power if we had it. If the disposition to study be necessary to intellectual development, then the want of that disposition seems to imply the want of mental powers, which are the things to be developed. But this is erroneous.

The sun will ripen all kinds of seeds, if placed in a proper position to receive the full influence of its rays.

That position does not depend on the sun, or on the seeds, but on a third something which we denominate opportunity. Now, education is nothing else than the act of affording this opportunity to the minds of the people. All will not and cannot profit by it equally; but all may profit to some extent, if they please. Some men's minds are like a small measure, while others are like the crater of a volcano; yet the small mind, when it is filled, will feel content, and the large one can do no more.

Connected with this subject, is the question of self-discipline and self-instruction. All men who have become great, have become great in this way. Others cannot enlarge your mind; though they may supply you with the materials and instruments, it is you who must use them. Intellectual power is like a magnet; it draws to itself all things which have any analogy with its nature. Iron lies unmoved by the common stone, but place it out thousands of miles upon the ocean, in a condition to declare its propensity, and it will tremble and quiver, and turn its magnetic point unerringly towards the north. So it is with the soul. All ideas that belong to it come to it like birds over the waters of the deluge to the ark. It is their natural home, and they find the way by attraction.

All the young men of Stratford-upon-Avon did

not write Hamlets and Macbeths, because they were not Shakespeares. Yet the gates of knowledge lay as open to them as to him. But the temple stood upon a height which they could not reach, while he mounted with Titanian tread, and took his place in it among the intellectual patricians of the world.

The same, in an inferior degree, is true of Jean-Jacques Rousseau. When he fled from Geneva, he knew less than most English schoolboys. But the sacred fire was in him, and, as he went along the earth, lighted his steps through poverty and want, through neglect and obscurity, through celebrity and infamy, towards one of those thrones of power which are the standing-places for the men who are meant by nature to move the world. Burns and Chatterton, Watt, Bolton, Franklin, and many others, have in the same manner, though with less splendour, forced their way up the toilsome acclivity of fame. It is to enable others possessing equal aptitude, to follow in the same track, that the State is now invited to supply, through taxation, the means of kindling up, or rather of diffusing, that influence which may call forth the genius that might otherwise be condemned to slumber in obscurity for ever.

To return to the subject of smattering, the ' Times '*

* There appeared in the ' Times,' during the past year, a series of

observes, that there is little danger of the adult labouring classes in this country, over-educating themselves :
but there is a danger, that, when they take up a book
of Geography, History, or Politics at odd hours, they
may become conceited, and fancy they know a great
deal more than they do.   But should they act thus,
they would by no means stand alone in their error.
We are all inclined to imagine we know a little more
than we do; so that at worst the labouring classes
would only resemble their betters.

able, suggestive, and polished articles on the subject of education,
which I once intended to request permission to print at the end of this
work ; but, upon examination, I found they were sufficiently numerous
to make a small volume of themselves.   It would be doing a public
service, to collect and publish them.

CHAPTER VII.

GEOGRAPHY.—DIFFERENT RACES OF MEN.—DISTRIBU-
TION OF PLANTS AND ANIMALS.

Vastness of Knowledge.—Germs of Civilization.—Creation of Pro-
perty. — Caverns.—Houses.—Villages.—Agriculture. — Course of
Streams.—Universal Diffusion of Culture.—Domestication of Ani-
mals.—Development of the Human Race.—The formation of Lan-
guages.—Invention of Writing.—Working Men.—Mechanics' Insti-
tutes.—Scantiness of Time.—Style of Travellers.—Light Reading.
—Preliminary to Better.—Ethnology.—Various Races of Men.—
Ethnological Institution.—Specimens of Tribes and Nations.—
Ancillary Studies.—Ethnological Maps.—Geography of Religions.
—Maps of Natural History and Botany.

Just now, however, we need not inquire by what
inconveniences the diffusion of education is likely to
be accompanied. The great object is to strengthen,
enlarge, and vivify the popular mind, which can only
be done by rendering knowledge irresistibly attractive.
In itself it is like the ocean, vast and unfathomable,
and, if contemplated in its infinity, calculated rather
to overawe and paralyze than stimulate the powers
of the mind. The soul must be brought into communion with it almost by stealth, through devious

and flowery ways, and not thrust out suddenly upon the shores of the measureless expanse. To allure the student forward, he must be shown not merely what may be useful, but what is pleasant and fitted to interest his newly awakened faculties, to excite his curiosity, and create the impression, that he becomes richer and richer in mental treasures at every step he takes in advance.

Geography, taken in its widest acceptation, is peculiarly adapted to accomplish this purpose. Being inhabitants of the earth, it is obviously incumbent upon us to cultivate some degree of acquaintance with as much of its surface as we can, with its animal and vegetable productions, with the way in which it has been divided and parcelled out among the several sections of the human family.

While engaged in considering these things, we find new questions springing up before us at every step. If we commence our view with the earth in a state of nature, we behold nothing on all sides but immense forests covering hills and plains, rivers forcing along their waters through uncertain channels; here spreading into reedy morasses, there rushing along in impetuous torrents, bearing upon their surface innumerable trunks of trees; here forming new islands, there destroying such as had been previously formed, and everywhere sending up noisome exhalations, big with disease and death.

In the woods, and along the margin of these rivers, animals of all kinds pursue or are pursued by each other, and by the imperial savage, man. Gradually, in fortunate spots, some natural impulse in the mind leads the human inhabitants to practise tillage. Certain grasses, having been found to bear nutritive seeds, are cultivated, and man enjoys the satisfaction of eating bread. Trees are cared for on account of their fruits, and spots of ground are enclosed to protect them from the larger and more destructive animals. The owners of these fields and orchards soon emerge from caverns, and erect themselves dwellings, either of timber or stone; and the foundation is thus laid of a hamlet, which by degrees becomes a village, a town, a city. Cultivation is pursued down to the margin of streams, which are taught to follow a fixed channel, until they roll into the depth of those capacious valleys which Nature herself has given them for their bed, and become mighty rivers. Next, we see meadows created, pasturage selected for sheep, fields of corn waving and presenting their golden bosoms to the sun, and, little by little, all the infinite processes of civilization, which are rapidly converting the surface of our planet into one garden of diversified beauty.

Connected with this subject, is the dispersion of the human race, and of all those animals which have accompanied it into every clime, amid every change of fortune; the horse, the ox, the sheep, the dog. In some countries, we find the elephant and the camel the allies or servants of man. Birds, too, at his bidding have abandoned the woods, to associate themselves with his fortunes. Thus the peacock, emerging from the forests of Northern India, has lent its gay plumage to adorn the farm-yard of the European yeoman; the cock has accompanied us northward from Media; the pheasant from the shores of the Black Sea; while the horse itself, from the burning wastes of Arabia, where its coat is short and shining, has put on long hair, and shrunk to almost half its original size, in order to share man's labours in the mountainous and frozen north.

The most interesting portion of geography, however, regards the movements and settlements of the human species, the formation of languages, the growth of empires, kingdoms, and commonwealths, and the transmission from place to place of that wonderful system by which, with infinite ingenuity, man has contrived to bestow permanent duration upon his thoughts. Other topics, scarcely less curious and prolific of reflection, arise out of a consideration of the structure and aspect of the earth's surface.

Against the practicability of working men's pursuing this study to any great length, strong objections may be urged. Many of these, however, disappear before the advantages supplied by rural libraries and mechanics' institutes. But the principal objection must always retain much of its force,—I mean the scantiness of time at their disposal. It is rarely found that gentlemen, with all appliances and means to boot, make any great proficiency in geography. What they do learn, they learn in a casual, unscientific manner, from books of travels and the occasional glimpses opened up into the physical condition of the world by history. It is not, consequently, to be expected that working men should pursue a more laborious course. On the contrary, we may fairly presume that their style of reading will be still more desultory and imperfect.

Travellers very often possess few attractions for the general reader. Their object appears to be to describe everything they see, from the cedar of Lebanon to the hyssop that springeth out of the wall. They are perhaps geologists, ethnologists, antiquarians, and fully resolved that no knowledge which they have been at the pains to acquire shall be thrown away. Among their acquisitions, the art of writing is frequently not numbered. They say what they have to say in an awkward, slovenly manner, destitute of warmth, vivacity, imagination, and all those graces and colours of style which beget an interest in the mind of the reader. People consequently speak of their works with respect, but nevertheless lay them speedily aside, to take up perhaps with some gossiping scribbler who knows little or nothing beyond the trick of creating an interest in his sketches. No matter. We are a light generation, and light writers will always find light readers. Besides, as I have said, when men have only odd hours or half-hours to spare, they naturally, and indeed almost necessarily, betake themselves to what used to be called royal roads to knowledge.

We have comic histories of England, and, without being so named, comic books of travels into various parts of the world. The writer begins joking in the title-page, and jokes to the end ; but if he went about with his eyes open, he could not fail to see something worth talking of, and if he talks pleasantly about that, he may be allowed to have done good service to the community. The light, trifling, shallow book finds its way into a Mechanics' Institute, and gets readers, many or few, according to the measure of entertainment it affords. The chances however are, that in several cases a desire may be created to know more concerning the country and people described than the comic traveller supplies.

Recourse is then had to writers of a more sober stamp, of greater depth, and superior industry; and thus, through jests, quips, cranks, and ludicrous exaggerations, people are accidentally led to familiarize themselves with some portion of the world.

We have only recently begun to apply ourselves to what is called ethnology, or that department of science which treats of the several divisions of the human family, their varieties of race, structure, mental development, tastes, and idiosyncrasies; yet how vast and interesting a field does this knowledge lay open before us! There are certain principles and modes of thinking, common to the whole human race; but, overstepping these, we soon arrive, in every country, at strange peculiarities of opinion, fantastic beliefs, superstitious moralities and manners, distinguishing one tribe or nation from another, more strikingly than rivers or ridges of mountains divide the lands they inhabit.

To become acquainted with the facts of this science is desirable for persons of all ranks, because such knowledge enlarges men's sympathies, while it ex-

pands and elevates their minds. In order however
to pursue this study with success, we should be
brought in contact with individuals belonging to the
several divisions of the human family. To accomplish this by travelling is impossible. The nation
therefore, if it wishes its own enlightenment, should
be at the cost of forming an ethnological institution,
with very extensive grounds, on which by degrees
might be located specimens in pairs of the various
races which could subsist in our climate.

They should construct their own dwellings according to the architectural ideas of their several countries; their furniture, dress, ornaments, amusements,
food, and mode of life, should be their own. The
forms of industry prevalent in their nation or tribe
they should be required to practise; and their ideas,
opinions, habits, and superstitions should be permitted
to perpetuate themselves until extinguished by the
spontaneous effects of civilization. The Esquimaux,
the Red Indian, the Caffre, the Hottentot, the Negro,
the Australian, the New Zealander, the Dyak, the
Malay, the wild Goond, the Cingalese, the Belouche,
the Afghan, the Brahmin, and various other castes
and tribes of India, might thus be brought together
within the same enclosure. In many ways, such an
assemblage would serve to throw light on the nature

and primitive ideas of our species; and not the least
instructive part of the plan would be the study of the
way in which civilization affected these several sections of mankind.

To go from one division of this establishment to
another would be like travelling into a new country;
and the student of languages might be able to investigate, in the most easy and favourable way, the almost
infinite modifications of human speech.   The creation
of such a school, however, would be much more practicable in a country like the United States, where the
territories are vast, and land is cheap, than here with
us in England, where every inch of soil is valuable.
Still, even among us, the thing would not be impossible.   Meanwhile by books, lectures, with maps and
engravings, we may convey to the minds even of the
humblest classes some idea of the varieties of the
human race, scattered over the surface of the globe.

We might perhaps commence—but the order
would not greatly signify—with exhibiting, upon
properly coloured maps, the distribution of the several
races. The countries inhabited by the Negroes might
be tinted nearly black; those in which people of
Mongol origin, such as the Chinese, Japanese, Ton-
quinese, and the Hindú Chinese nations generally,
might be coloured yellow; the territories of the

people of the Semitic race, as the Arabs and Persians, might be dyed brown; those of the North
American Indians, red; those of the Esquimaux,
Laplanders, and Samoiedes, blue; while the lands of
the Caucasian race, Europeans, and Hindús, might
be permitted to retain upon the map their original
virgin white.*

Another series of maps might be constructed to
illustrate the distribution of religions; Protestantism,
Catholicism, Mohammedanism, and Paganism in all
its marvellous varieties. If we adopted white for the
colour of our own faith, we should be deeply afflicted
to observe how small a space it would occupy in the
map of the world. Still we should derive some comfort
from the knowledge that it is always on the increase;
that it is spreading slowly, but irresistibly, over one
tract after another, while all the opposing creeds have
their limits necessarily contracted in the same proportion. Had a map of the world been drawn upon this
principle eighteen hundred and fifty years ago, there
would not have been one white spot upon its surface.
Another century would have shown streaks of light,
penetrating, here and there, on the confines of Western Asia, and in Europe, amidst every variety of

* See the map appended to 'L'Homme: Essai Zoologique sur le
Genre Humain; par M. Bory de Saint-Vincent.'

dusky shade. At the end of four centuries the white would have been greatly diffused, and so on, down to our own day.

El Islam, the religion of the sword, marked with red, would vindicate to itself a considerable portion of the earth's surface; but Brahmanism, with the religions which have sprung from it, would cover by far the largest portion of the thickly peopled divisions of the world. In like manner might be illustrated the distribution of animals, the camel, the elephant, the horse; remarkable vegetable productions, such as the palm, the grape, wheat, the sugar-cane, and so on. In this way, it appears to me, the minds of the people might be imbued with truly useful knowledge.

CHAPTER VIII.

PHILOSOPHY OF EXTINCT RELIGIONS.

Religious Instinct.—Idea of Immortality.—Pinnacles of the Physical and Intellectual Worlds.—Origin of Ancient Religions.—Mythology.—Lord Bacon.—Mental Condition of Antiquity.—The Ni and the Noon People.—Fables depicted on the visible Heavens.—Mythology of the Poets.—Milton.—Shakespeare.—Traces of Greek and Roman Thought.—The English pre-eminently Religious and Poetical.—Songs and Ballads of our Ancestors.

CONNECTED with this part of the subject there is a branch of study which, at first sight, perhaps, may appear too abstruse ever to become popular. But I am not of this opinion. I allude to the history of the rise and progress of religious ideas among mankind. An old philosopher observed, most justly, that man is a religious animal. Account for it how we please, it is certain that he must and will have something to worship,—the true God if he can discover Him, and if not, false gods of some kind or another. The manner in which this instinct has developed itself from the beginning, must surely be interesting to all who recognize the highest powers and qualities of our nature. That we are meant to live for a time, among the other animals, upon the surface of this globe, is of course obvious to every one.

But men no sooner began to reflect upon their own situation, than they conceived the idea of an existence resumed after it had been interrupted by death. I do not undertake to explain how this idea originated, or whence it came, but it is undeniable that it is fixed and ineradicable in the whole human race. It, in fact, forms the basis of the intellectual life of our species, and appears to be the link which connects our animal nature with a nature which—call it what we please—is not animal. This nature it is that, by its growth and development, has enabled us to emerge from the woods, to build cities, to organize States and Commonwealths, and to elevate the human understanding to something like a divine level.

The physical world has its Alps, its Andes, and its Himalayas, upon which the day-spring from on high first alights, when it emerges from the chambers of the east. On those pinnacles, therefore, it is day long before the valleys and plains become conscious of the approach of light. It is much the same with the summits of the intellectual world, which rise and pierce the heavens and commune with them long, very long, before the vast level masses of humanity can be made partakers of divine truth. But in some sense, those lofty intellects are only so many channels to convey the blessing down to the other divisions of mankind.

It must be interesting to learn how this process began, and was carried on among the nations of old; what notions they entertained of God and nature, and how they became sensible of the duties growing out of our relations with the invisible Power or Powers, according to the theories they adopted. Knowledge like this can assuredly never be considered dry or uninteresting, unless it be rendered so by the way in which it is conveyed. Many persons may perhaps object that the study of obsolete mythologies is little calculated to improve the mind, because they were only so many bundles of errors. But myths, if properly comprehended, will never be found to have been mere errors: they were but fabulous dresses put on by Truth. This was the light in which Lord Bacon considered them, and not one of the least curious of his productions is an attempt to extract from portions of the ancient mythology the wisdom it contains.

We often suffer ourselves to be cheated by words, and turned away, through prejudices and false shame, from pursuits which experience would have proved to

be beneficial. It is only necessary for us, when we undertake to examine such things as the religions and
myths of extinct nations, to understand clearly what
we are in search of. We do not want to discover something to believe, but to find out, if we can, what, in
very different states of civilization, other communities
of men did once believe, as well as why they believed
it. We cannot doubt that they had faculties like our
own, and were perhaps quite as logical. It was only
the condition of their existence that was different.

Supposing a number of individuals to be condemned to form a judgment of the aspect of nature,
during the hour which precedes the dawn; would
they not form false or imperfect conceptions of most
objects, and fall into a number of extravagant errors?
The individuals who came afterwards to review their
theories and notions by the light of the mid-day sun,
would be able, no doubt, to detect innumerable mis-
takes But the before-day people and the noon people
might be, one every whit as wise as the other. The
only difference between them would be the accident
of the hour. No blame would attach to the former
for being born before the sun was up, and no merit to
the latter for being born afterwards. However, the
people of the light may be allowed to experience some
curiosity to learn what those who flourished before

it rose, thought and believed of the world and its Maker.

Besides, the fables of those remote ages are written in undying characters on the visible heavens, and on the still more vast and enduring heaven of the human mind. We cannot take a walk after dark without feeling the power of the religion of the old world deep in our souls. Scarcely a star glitters on the face of night, which does not figure in some myth or legend. Orion and Boötes, Cassiopeia and the Pleiades, rise up in brightness before us, while Argo pursues its eternal voyage towards Colchis.

Again, all poetical literature is drenched to saturation with ideas derived from the Mythology. Without some acquaintance, therefore, with the fables in which they first made their appearance, we cannot enjoy the beauty of the noblest and most perfect creations of human genius. Milton, from the extent and variety of his learning, might naturally enough be expected to abound in mythological allusions; and to follow him in imagination, is to revivify every moment the beliefs and opinions of long past generations. Shakespeare was not, in the ordinary sense, a man of learning. In him, accordingly, judging beforehand, we might be disposed to look for much fewer traces of admiration for the old fables. The fact, however, is quite otherwise, since Shakespeare deals far more lavishly even than Milton with ideas and allusions derived from classical springs. The wings of his fancy appear to have been always wet with spray from the Castalian fount. He revelled above all men in the exhaustless riches of the Mythology, which accordingly sparkle over his writings as thickly as stars in the Milky Way.

There is, however, no poet or great prose writer whose conceptions can be fully appreciated without some acquaintance with the history of ancient religions. Take Bacon, Hobbes, Burke, Bossuet, or Fénelon, and you will be able to advance but a little way without stumbling over some fragment of Greek or Roman thought intimately connected with outworn religions; nay, the least educated writers, men who never planted wrinkles in their forehead by poring over Plato, Thucydides, Aristotle, always contrive to catch at second-hand some faint colours from that glorious rainbow which spanned the ancient world, and shed hues so rich and gorgeous over the minds of its inhabitants.

I may be wrong, but it certainly appears to me, that the people of this country have a peculiar aptitude for receiving and appreciating all ideas connected with the progress of religion, whether false or true. This probably may account for the prodigious prevalence and efficacy of poetry among us. Nowhere, perhaps, was there ever found, if we except Greece alone, a greater body of metrical compositions. In the very rudest ages, all branches of our ancestors, Britons, Scandinavians, Saxons, were remarkable for their hymns, their ballads, their songs, and romances; and at this day, among the least educated of our population, we discover a fondness for uncouth rhymes, which pass from mouth to mouth, and from age to age, embodying the maxims of prudence, together with the fancies or the superstitions of their authors and their neighbours.

CHAPTER IX.

INFLUENCE OF RELIGION ON EDUCATION.

Claims of the Clergy honourable to them, but inadmissible.—Sure
Foundation of Human Happiness.—Great Heirloom of Mankind.—
Self-dependence and Integrity.—Religion the basis of Liberty.—
Strange idea of Volney.—The Druzes.—Profound Faith of the
Brave.—Our Puritan Forefathers.—General Havelock.—The Spar-
tans of the Modern World.—Infidelity and National Extinction.
—The Teachers of Religion.—Secular Knowledge.—Forgetfulness
of God.—The Peace of the Soul.—Difficulty of Religious Teaching.
—Public Worship.—The Bible.—Spirit of Society.—No fear of
Irreligion.—Singular opinion of Mr. Henley.—Theology and Ethics.
—The most vast and difficult of Studies.—All Crime Ignorance.

GROWING naturally out of those considerations, is
the topic upon which, of all those connected with
education, it is the most hazardous and difficult to
touch. It will at once be seen that I mean Religion.
The word is no sooner pronounced, than a host of
oppositions, antagonisms, and discords spring up
around it. The question is immediately asked, " Who
is to teach it,—Catholic or Protestant, the Church
of England or Dissenters ?" Each section of the

Clergy * comes forward at once and demands to be entrusted by the State with the disciplining and storing of the minds of our youth.

Some blame them for this, but, in my opinion, unjustly. It is perfectly natural that, exactly in proportion to the force of their own convictions, they should be eager to impart them to others. This

---

* To the honour of the Clergy it should be remembered, that they have, in all ages and countries, done more than any other class of men towards the diffusion of knowledge and the development of the powers of the mind. The Monks also of the Roman Church have been indefatigable in their educational labours, to which every portion of the world, civilized or uncivilized, must bear testimony. Ranke supplies one illustration of this truth, which deserves to be introduced here. "Upper Italy, " he says, "had been visited, since the year 1521, with continual war, and in its train with desolation, famine, and disease. How many children were there made orphans, and threatened with ruin in body and soul! Happily, pity dwells among men, close by misfortune. A Venetian senator, Girolamo Miani, gathered together the children who were fugitives in Venice, and received them in his house, seeking them out, through the islands and the city. Without paying much heed to the scolding of his sister-in-law, he sold his plate, and the handsomest tapestry in his house, to procure for the children lodging, food, raiment, and instruction. By degrees he devoted his whole energy to this vocation. His success was particularly great in Bergamo. The hospital which he founded there was so strenuously supported, that he was encouraged to make similar experiments in other towns. By-and-by hospitals of the same kind were established at Verona, Brescia, Ferrara, Como, Milan, Pavia, and Genoa. Finally, he entered with some friends of like sentiments into a congregation of regular Clergy, modelled on that of the Theatines, designated by the name Di Somasca. Their main object was education. Their hospitals received a common constitution."

therefore on their part is only an additional title to our respect.   Still, as what they aim at is impossible, they must not feel hostile towards the State for pursuing its own course and rejecting their claims. They maintain, with the greatest truth, that of all the subjects which can occupy the human mind, religion is infinitely the most momentous.   It is not simply the cornerstone of all our acquisitions, it is the only foundation upon which human happiness, here and hereafter, can be erected.   I will go further, and contend that no study is beautiful or satisfying or comforting, considered altogether apart from religion. This therefore every man ought to regard as his birthright, his peculiar property, the great heir-loom of himself and his race.

If it were possible, I would commence all education with pouring into the mind those vital ideas which, growing with its growth, and strengthening with its strength, must ultimately impart to it integrity, self-dependence, and moral grandeur, contentment upon the hearth, independence in the world, the love of justice, and the love of liberty.

An irreligious people can never be independent or great or free.   Volney once made the strange remark that the Druzes of Mount Lebanon did not fear or hesitate to die, because they had no belief in the immortality of the soul. But it was precisely because they had such belief that they did not fear. All believers in immortality are fearless in the field of battle, fearless in council, fearless everywhere. Persuaded that nothing can destroy them, they are ever ready to uphold the right at the peril of their mortal lives.

In proof of this, we have but to turn back a few pages in our own history, and consider our Puritan ancestors. The bravest Spartans in Sparta's best days, the warriors of Marathon, the legions of the Roman Republic when it stood up in arms against the world, were not more intrepid or utterly regardless of death than the soldiers of Naseby and Marston Moor. They felt that they were fighting at once for their civil liberty and their faith, and laid down their lives as cheerfully as the holiest martyrs of our religion. But this they would never have done, had they believed for one moment that their souls would go out, like so many candles, on the gory field. They laid down their lives because they believed they should take them up again amid eternal splendours in another world. Such was their persuasion; and the liberty, the civilization, the political power, the superiority over all other nations, which we now enjoy, are the fruits of that persuasion.

The civil war in India has supplied numerous proofs that the same religious spirit still pervades the English people. General Havelock, who has left behind him so enviable a reputation, was only the representative of a large class of British officers who emulated his bravery, his piety, and his patriotism, and who, when they fall, if fall they must, will leave behind them names scarcely less dear to England. A writer, transmitting home an account of the feelings with which the deceased General is remembered by his surviving comrades in arms, says: " He was a slight spare man, about five feet five inches in height, with an emaciated face, and an eagle eye. He belonged emphatically to the class who have never to contend with disobedience or mutiny. As a General, he was the best tactician we have had in India; and as an officer, though stern and sometimes exacting, his antique heroism made him the idol of his men. He was indeed, perhaps, the bravest man in his own army, and was never so chatty or agreeable as under fire. Like most of our Indian statesmen and soldiers, the Lawrences, Edwardes, Nicholsons, Montgomeries, and many others, he was a Christian of the old stamp, a strong, God-fearing, Puritan man, who thought often in Scriptural phrase, and deemed it no shame to teach his soldiers to pray. 'Turn out the Saints,' said Lord Gough, on one occasion, when he anticipated desperate work; 'Have-lock never blunders, and his men are never drunk.''*

It will be a woful day for the English race, when the belief in immortality ceases to actuate it. There will be no more liberty, no more greatness, no more growth of dominion. We-shall shrink, and dwindle, and pass away from the face of the earth, like so many other nations that have died out in infidelity and baseness, and the place that knew us shall know us no more for ever.

It will not then be supposed that I undervalue the teaching of religion to the people. But who are to be their teachers? The protestant clergy come forward and maintain it must be they, and the catholic clergy do the same. Nay, the ministers of every sect insist upon the privilege of imparting spiritual instruction to their own congregations. This circumstance has driven a large number of the advocates of popular education to the expedient of confining school instruction to secular knowledge; and, however much we may lament it, there seems to be no other choice left. One satisfaction, however, we must have, namely, that all kinds of pure knowledge lead directly and inevitably to religion.

I am perfectly aware, in certain moods of vanity,

* 'Times,' January 13th, 1858.

men think they can do well enough without God, and accordingly forget him as completely as they can. We do much the same, however, with nearly all God's gifts. We never practically know we have eyes, till they begin to fail us; or health, till we are touched by disease. Knowledge itself is only thought to be divine, when we are tortured by the pangs of ignorance. It is much the same with religion. We can get on wonderfully well without it when we are prosperous and in good health, while the world smiles upon us, and when we have nothing to do but to enjoy ourselves. But with the first cloud that passes over our prospects, we begin to feel the want of something which fortune cannot supply, of something situated in the mind itself, altogether beyond the reach of time, and chance, and misfortune, and adversity. If we have such a possession, we are able to bear up against the ills of life; if not, we sink and die.

There may be those who experience pleasure in thinking differently, partly perhaps because they have seen religion deformed and mutilated, and presented to them in ghastly colours. But this is not the fault of the thing itself, but of the way in which people mangle it. Properly considered, religion is that inward tranquillity, harmony, contentment, which the Scriptures describe as "the peace of God which passeth all understanding." It is peace, peace with God above and with man below; above all things, it is peace with ourselves.

The more excellent, however, and necessary this knowledge is proved to be, the more earnestly do those who feel its worth desire to enjoy the privilege of imparting it to the people. But whatever may be the strength of their zeal or the benevolence of their disposition, they must consent to look fairly in the face all the difficulties by which the subject is surrounded. All sections of the clergy, it is clear, cannot enjoy such a privilege. Is it not better therefore that none should? In a Christian country, the children may surely be expected to attend some place of worship on Sundays; and if the doctrines and practices of Christianity be then intelligibly and forcibly explained, they will thus be made acquainted with the basis and character of their religion.

Besides, the Bible is always at hand, cheap, portable, and accessible to every man, in his own language; language earnest, simple, and beautiful, calculated even by its own charms to win people over to the truths it teaches.

Moreover, the pervading spirit of society in these islands is inevitably more or less Christian. Everybody is aware that he is not a Mohammedan or a Hindù, a Buddhist or a Fetish worshipper. Children cannot fail to inquire of their parents, of their friends, of their companions, Who was Christ? and, though the answer they receive may not always be very satisfactory, still it is difficult to imagine that as knowledge enlarges its empire, it should be able to spread fast and far without revealing to the soul, however darkly or dimly, the way to Calvary.

I take it for granted, therefore, that Christianity must and will make its way among us in proportion to our general enlightenment; and such being my conviction, I do not hesitate to accept a secular system of education, provided it be not based upon irreligion, of which I presume there is little danger. The Dean of Hereford, one of the great ornaments of the Church to which he belongs, has a passage on this subject which is so excellent and so much to the purpose, that I cannot resist the pleasure of introducing it here. "There are some, I fear, who oppose secular education as unfitted for the labouring classes, and would have all instruction confined to religious teaching, or a very little beyond this.

"Now, I cannot see how religion can be *well* taught, without the secular element being mixed with it. For instance, take a Christian working man. If he be enlightened as a Christian, he must feel that he has a duty to perform to his employer. He has made an engagement; he ought to fulfil that engagement in the best possible manner, that is, to the utmost of his ability; and how can he do so, unless he apply himself to understand the nature of the work he has in hand? This can only be gained by secular instruction; whether he be an agricultural labourer, a mechanic, or tradesman in any of the arts of life.

"And now, let me draw your attention to the working man's recreations. How sweet is rest after earnest, well-directed labour!

"Ought we not to endeavour to make that rest, not only sweet, but elevating to his mind, by giving him an interest in all those beautiful and useful objects with which our beneficent Creator has surrounded us, from the tiny flower, so lovely that its picture is seen on the most costly ornaments that decorate a monarch's dwelling, to the noble oak, which outlives many generations of men, yet, by man's skill, the gift of God, is worked up into the stately frigate. Think, again, of the mineral world—of minerals, too, how beautiful they are in their varied uses; of that common mineral, coal, for instance, what comfort it brings, what enlarged facilities in traversing the globe; of the electric wire,

—up to the glorious orb of heaven, with the moon
and stars walking their courses by the command of
their and our great Creator.

"Surely no Christian is justified in withholding a
knowledge, however slight, of such things from his
fellow-man, endowed with the same capacity that he
himself has. Nay, is he not rather bound by the
holiest ties of brotherhood to encourage its acquisition? And is not this a vast field of secular instruction."

Milton has observed with equal boldness and wisdom, that wherever truth happens to be in the field,
we need not much fear the arms or the power of
error. Bacon says of some men, that they love the
lie for the lie's sake, and not because of any profit
it brings them. But this can hardly be predicated
of a whole nation, especially when grandeur and
meanness, piety and impiety, happiness and misery,
are in the balance.

Let us trust for this to the common sense of mankind, who, though they have wandered long in darkness, must be admitted, even from the very strides we
behold Christianity making among them, to prefer
the true religion to the false.

I cannot consequently share the apprehensions of
Lord Ravensworth and Mr. Henley, who would al-

most appear to think that the understandings of the people had better be left uncultivated. In the debate on Sir John Pakington's motion, (February 18, 1857,) Mr. Henley observed, "I know it is said that, unless persons possess a great deal of secular knowledge, your labour in attempting to give them religious instruction, is thrown away. (Cries of hear, hear, in which Sir J. Pakington was understood to join.) My right hon. friend cheers that statement. I am sorry to hear him cheer it. All I can say is, that I differ from that opinion as much as light differs from darkness. I do not believe that the most ignorant man who ever drew the breath of heaven, was not amenable to the truths of Christianity. Those who have had the most extensive experience on this point, will tell you that the best examples of a truly Christian spirit are often furnished by the most illiterate of our fellow-creatures. The divine message of mercy to man, is so wonderfully adapted to the wants of man, that while the humble peasant can understand and receive its gracious accents, the highly intellectual, and most cultivated of our race, will esteem it their greatest privilege to submit themselves to its lessons of humility. If you assert that our duty to God and man is to be sought only through the intellect, you have only arrived, as the result of seven years of discussion, at what you might easily have seen from the beginning was the radical difference between us. I say, that you must invert the process. You must first teach our duty to God and man, and, as a consequence of that teaching, induce people to cultivate their intellects according as their means and opportunities enable them."

Mr. Henley's notions on this subject appear to be somewhat confused. The science which teaches us our duty towards God is theology, while that which instructs us in our duty towards man is ethics. Are we to begin the education of children by pouring into their minds the truths contained in these vast and sublime departments of human knowledge? Can we commence the study of any science, without possessing in a proper condition the instrument by which alone we can conduct such study? This instrument is intellect, and therefore the training and disciplining of the intellect must obviously precede all other processes. When the mind is dark, weak, or filled with prejudices and superstitions, the first step towards enlightening and clearing it, is to strengthen the faculty by which that enlightening and clearing can be alone effected.

The thing signified by our duty towards God, is

highly complex and difficult of comprehension. It is
necessary first to build up the idea of what God is ;
next, we must place before the mind the mighty act
of creation ; then we must show the nature of our
own being in every sense of the word, dependent,
weak, when regarded by itself, powerful and almost
divine, when considered as an emanation from God,
subsisting by His breath, and energizing under His
influence.

If the imparting of this knowledge seems easy to
Mr. Henley, I confess it appears the very reverse to
me. Again, our duty towards man. What is it?
Does it not spread out into infinite ramifications?
What else but the theories of our duty to each
other are we learning all our lives ?   Has not human
society, from its very commencement, been engaged
perpetually in the attempt to discover what men
ought to do in the infinitely multiplied circumstances
of life ?

For myself, I agree with Plato, that all irreligion,
all crime—everything by which we can suppose ourselves to offend God or injure our neighbours,—is
ignorance. If, when about to perpetrate any act of
wickedness, a man were careful to enlighten himself
respecting all its bearings, present, and future, he
would certainly never commit it.   He would see that

in every possible situation in life, it is better to do
what is right than what is wrong. We never undertake anything, but with a view to improve our condition. If therefore, by the force of intellect, we
could place ourselves, while innocent, in the situation
in which we must inevitably be when we have become guilty, we should shrink with unspeakable horror
from the meditated act. It is because we are thought-
less, it is because we take false views—in one word,
it is because we are ignorant—that we commit crimes
and withhold from God that profound adoration of
the soul which is not more his due than it is our
happiness to pay it. Consequently, when we reflect
into what guilt and impiety we are betrayed by ignorance, we must surely be deeply solicitous to deliver
ourselves from this most pernicious and besetting sin
of our nature.

CHAPTER X.

THE AFFECTIONS AND DOMESTIC VIRTUES.

Rousseau.—Molière.—Lord Robert Cecil.—Education of the Heart.
—Reasoning in a Circle.—Home and School Teaching.—Affection,
Innate.—Developed and Directed by Training.—Children of the
Poor.—Discipline of Misfortune.—Education of Women.—Accomplishments of the Rich.—Mischievous to the Poor.—What a Woman
ought to know.—Schools of Housewifery.—Well and Ill-ordered
Dwellings.—Female Neatness. — Natural Qualities of Women.—
Domestic Virtues of our Ancestors. — The Peasant Women of
France.—Their becoming Costume. — Their Cleanliness and In-
dustry.—Their Superior Cooking. — The Cabarets.—Manners of
the Peasants.—Rustic Ignorance.—The Legislature.—The Ladies
of England.—Female Servants.—Bad System of Training.—Efforts
of Clergymen.—Domestic Economy.—The Nation's Duty.—Art of
Talking. — Oriental Story-tellers. — Memory of the Illiterate.—
Anecdote.— Slovenliness and Discomfort.—Women of Egypt and
France. — False Notions of Women.—How they should be instructed.

JEAN Jacques Rousseau, who had profoundly studied
the art of forming the character, both of individuals
and nations, maintains that the object of education is
to discipline the heart, the judgment, and the understanding of youth. He attaches the greatest impor-

tance to the regulation of the affections; next in order, comes the strengthening of the judgment; and lastly, the improvement and conduct of the understanding. Many teachers appear to imagine that education entirely consists, not in enlarging and strengthening the mind, but in filling it with a knowledge of the sciences. Rousseau, however, adopts the opinion of Molière, that an ignorant fool is much more tolerable than an educated one, because, while the former can only exhibit his folly on but a few subjects, the latter can play the fool on almost everything.

In what regards the affections, Lord Robert Cecil agrees entirely with Rousseau. "To educate the young," he says, " is really not so much to cultivate their intellects as it is to train their hearts, to mould their habits of feeling and of action in accordance with the precepts of religion. The culture of the memory and the reason, which is the work of the schoolmaster, is not education. Real education cannot be done on the school bench, under terror of the school cane, by help of school books and black board. If done at all, it must be done elsewhere than at school. It must be the result of the influences which breathe around the daily life in a well-ordered home; of a mother's affectionate care and tender vigilance;

of holy lessons instilled and fostered under the genial warmth of that soft religious sympathy which speaks not in catechisms, but from heart to heart; of that which teaches more than words can teach—the daily example of a parent's virtuous life. So far as these exist, the child will have a real education. If this were general, we should indeed effect what we seek in vain from our school instruction—the extirpation of profligacy and crime."*

These are manly and generous sentiments; but the logic they imply is extremely defective. Lord Robert Cecil certainly expects improvements to be made in our moral condition; and yet, if his reasoning be sound, all progress is impossible. It maintains that the affections are not to be developed and disciplined by school teaching; but he cannot otherwise than confess that innumerable children require to be trained in morality, virtue, and religion, whose parents are neither religious, virtuous, nor moral.

It is perfectly clear that parents cannot impart to their children what they themselves do not possess.†

* 'Times,' November 11th, 1856.

† Sir John Pakington, in a speech delivered at Manchester, observes that Mr. Unwin, in the House of Commons, employed much the same logic with Lord Robert Cecil. According to him, the State ought not to educate the children of the poor, because this is the sacred duty of parents. Practically, however, we find that parents do not perform their duty, for the most part because they do not

They are therefore in exactly the same condition, as far as training and discipline are concerned, as the school teachers, and consequently the children cannot be trained, disciplined, or improved at all. Of course Lord Robert Cecil does not in so many words affirm all this, but the consequences flow necessarily from what he does affirm. When parents are what they ought to be, they are the best teachers their children can possibly have. When the reverse is the case, the children must obviously depend for improvement entirely on school teaching. No form of instruction can impart affection. That is innate. All that others can do for us, is to aid in developing it, to direct it into proper channels, to keep it pure, and to connect it with high principles, agreeable manners, and a knowledge of its uses and purposes. If this view be correct, schoolmasters and schoolmistresses may do what is required for the children of the poor in England.

In order to impart force and efficacy to all kinds of teaching, there must be an early training and disciplining of the heart and affections, as well as of the

know what it is. Mr. Unwin, therefore, also adopts the circular style of reasoning, contending, that the State must not educate, because it is the duty of parents; while parents cannot, because they don't know how. From which it follows obviously, that the children of the English poor must remain for ever in ignorance.

mind. Intellect, considered by itself, is a cold principle. It dominates everything, but sympathizes with
nothing. To render it an instrument of human happiness, it must be steeped in emotion, it must be
engrafted upon love, it must be touched and softened
by sorrow.

The children of the poor, in this respect at least,
may be said to possess some advantages over others.
They are early acquainted with suffering, with privation, with self-sacrifice; and if the influence of the
hearth be pure and holy, they may, by their very
misfortunes, be led to cultivate many of those virtues
which are the greatest sources of happiness to mankind. What, then, is the first step towards inaugura-
ting this training and disciplining? It is to educate
women, the mothers of future generations, with whom,
if with any one, the improvement of society must
begin.

The opulent classes here, as elsewhere, prefer accomplishments, dash, show, glitter, to everything
else. With their education, therefore, I have in this
place nothing whatever to do; I speak of the poor.
Let them beware of accomplishments. The whole
science of a humble Englishwoman is included in the
knowledge how to make her husband and her children
happy. To insure this, she need neither sing nor play

music, nor dance, nor speak the tongues of foreign
nations. Let her be a good wife, a good mother, a
good nurse, a good cook, and take a delight in cleanliness and her home. Among her first studies ought
to be how to make and mend, and how, in all respects,
to order her little household so as to avoid confusion,
discord, and those heart-burnings which always arise
when duties small or great are neglected.

To promote the growth of home happiness, schools
of housewifery, like that of Miss Martineau at Norwich, should be multiplied, where girls might be
taught to sew, to cut out,* to cook plainly, to bake

* Mrs. Austin, in her Letters on Girls' Schools, (p. 27) observes, that
"a lady who resides in Leeds, struck with the wretched ignorance of
all womanly works in which the factory-girls grew up, has collected
them of an evening, for the purpose of making and mending their
clothes under her direction. My informant saw between seventy and
eighty of them occupied in this way. Their benevolent instructress
devotes to this work two evenings in every week. What is still more
remarkable, she is accompanied by her husband, who enters in a book
the orders of the girls, and keeps an account against each. Whatever they order, is carried the next evening, cut out, and prepared for
them to make. These admirable people have for years left the comforts of an opulent fireside, to pass their evenings in one of the lowest
parts of a manufacturing city, and in the society of factory-girls."
The Rev. Mr. Bruce, of Bristol, has set on foot a scheme for improving and elevating a much humbler class of young women—the
Orange and Willow-Girls. Several ladies, from motives of kindness
to the poor, devote some evenings in the week to the instruction of
these girls. At first they were found very intractable and disorderly ;
but by patience and forbearance they have been taught properly to
appreciate what is done for them. They are instructed in cutting

bread, and generally to be careful and economical.
There are a thousand things to be learned in the
management of a house, which cannot be conveyed by
writing, which cannot even be taught by speaking,
but must be inculcated by constant practice. All good
housewives know this well. By way of illustration,
let any one who has the least doubt on the subject
step successively into an ill-ordered and a well-ordered
cottage, supported by the same expense, and whose
inmates enjoy much the same advantages. It will become evident at once that in one the wife is prudent,
thoughtful, industrious, fond of her husband and her
home, and in the other that she is the reverse,—
slatternly, idle, gossiping, perhaps not too much addicted to sobriety.

I say nothing in this place of the husband. Let
him be good or bad, the wife will impress her own
character upon the interior of the house. No degree
of poverty can altogether annihilate a woman's neatness, cleanliness, and love of order. If she possess
but a few three-legged stools, a poor table, and a
scanty array of earthenware, she will somehow contrive to make the room she inhabits clean and tidy;

out, sewing, mending, and other domestic arts, in addition to reading
and writing. Some of their number have already obtained good
situations, and proved useful and obedient servants ; but there, as
everywhere else, the want of adequate employment for women is
painfully felt.

the spirit of arrangement will be visible; her own person will be sweet, and her whole appearance calculated to inspire respect.

No doubt good qualities in women as well as in men are, in the first instance, the gift of nature, and can be implanted by no training; but, perhaps, if we examine the matter narrowly, we shall find that they exist in a greater or less degree in all human beings. Indeed, to lack altogether any one quality of our nature, would be not to belong to that nature. Whatever is necessary to constitute a man or a woman, all men and women must obviously have. The differences perceived to exist are only in degree. In schools of housewifery it is to be presumed that all girls might be taught to be neat, careful, and orderly. This kind of training need not interfere with the imparting of ordinary instruction. Everybody in a civilized country should be able to read and write; but these acquirements are not to be put in competition with the cultivation of the domestic virtues. It is far more important that a girl should know how to make her own clothes, than that she should be able to enjoy a novel; that she should know how to nurse a baby, than that she should be able to sing a song or dance a quadrille; that she should understand how to make a bright hearth, than that she should be skilled in all the arts of gossip and all the mysteries of scandal. In these matters it appears to me that we are much less wise than our ancestors. They did at all events, as a rule, attend to the comforts, the conveniences, and consequently to the peace and happiness of their dwellings. As far as we can discover by the aid of history, much greater stress was laid in former times on the knowledge of household affairs, though, even now, in many parts of England the same good old homely virtues are held in veneration. The great point therefore is, to render them more general, to give them fresh strength where they are in activity, and to call them forth where they are still latent.

In many parts of France, where other kinds of instruction are very deficient, I have found the women of the poor, models of cleanliness and industry. They do not dress or live like women of the same class among us. There is no attempt at tawdry finery, not the slightest effort to imitate the fashions of the capital, or even of the small gentry of the neighbourhood. The peasants are content to dress like peasants, and preserve religiously the forms and fashions of the different garments they wear, as they have been handed down to them from former times. The woman's cap of today is a fac-simile of the cap worn by women of her class in the reign of Louis XI. It is the same with her boddice, her kerchief, her petticoat, her stockings, her wooden shoes. Her linen, though coarse, is, as Chaucer expresses it, " white as morrow milk," and turned down over the bright boddice five or six inches, like the " barm " of our great poet.

Almost without exception, these female peasants understand cookery, and make savoury dishes for their husbands such as men of a very superior class scarcely ever taste in other countries. As you walk by their cottage doors, when they are preparing their meals, you smell a wholesome and agreeable odour. The interior of their dwellings is very clean, and their children, however numerous, are almost invariably dressed in strong serviceable clothes, neatly made or carefully mended.

Accordingly, the cabarets are not frequented as with us. On Sundays and holidays the poor man takes his wife and children out into the fields, with a good basket of provisions and a bottle of cheap wine, with which they regale themselves in a homely and simple manner. Of course there are thousands who lead a different life; but, as a rule, the manners of the peasants in all the Departments of France with which I am acquainted, are marked by a primitive simplicity, cleanliness, sobriety, and contentment.

In what we call knowledge, they are extremely deficient; a majority can neither read nor write, and know very little of the world beyond their own village or commune. They go to church exactly as their forefathers went before them; they believe what they hear, and are very much afraid of giving offence to the priest, who often is not much less simple than they are.

This, I presume, is the sort of ignorance Mr. Henley thinks favourable to religion, and if philosophy were consulted on the subject, I make no doubt that it would give the preference to such ignorance, over the impudent acquisitions of dissipated and sensual worldlings.   It would say with Theseus:

> "In the modesty of fearful duty
> I read as much as from the rattling tongue
> Of saucy and audacious eloquence."

Still, since there is no necessary connection between ignorance and innocence, any more than between knowledge and criminality, it seems better that people should perform their duties because they know such performance to be conducive to their happiness, than through the mere force of habit.   Uninstructed persons more easily yield to temptation, than they who understand the nature of actions and consequences.

To carry out this reform in the education of the

poor, it is, I am persuaded, only necessary that the
Legislature should organize some plan, and the ladies
of England will of themselves put it in practice.   No
complaint is more common than that servants are
bad, though perhaps in some cases the fault lies in
the mistresses.   But allow them to be unequal to
their situations, with whom lies the blame?   Not
with the mistresses, certainly; but with the system of
female training prevalent in this country.   We will
not be at the pains to sow the seed, and yet irration-
ally hope to reap the harvest.   How can we expect
the poor to be acquainted with their duties, if nobody will be at the pains to teach them?

In some parishes here in London, I have known
clergymen, with their wives and daughters, almost
wear themselves out in the attempt to infuse a knowledge of domestic economy into the poor women of
their parishes.   They have visited every house; they
have talked long and earnestly with the inmates; they
have endeavoured to awaken industry by emulation,
by scolding, by praise, by gifts, by promises.   It
would be wrong to say that all this noble exertion
has been entirely thrown away; but yet they have
been in most cases forced into the conclusion, that
nothing of moment is to be done without early
training.

Schools, therefore, have been established, and proved of incalculable advantage in many points of view. The mind has been enlarged, the morals purified and elevated, but still the great point has not been achieved, because, in the schools at present existing, comparatively little attention is paid to the practice of domestic economy. Here and there, I believe, upon a small scale, an attempt has been made to supply the deficiency; but such efforts can make no impression upon the great body of the female poor. The task must be undertaken by the Nation, and in a manner worthy of the Nation's greatness; worthy of our civilization, of the faith we profess, and of the position we hold in the world.

It may appear, at first sight, something like a paradox, if not like a satire, to say that women should be taught to talk. Yet it is often for the want of this accomplishment that they drive their husbands to the public-house. Being uninstructed, the man and woman find nothing to say to each other. Having exhausted all the ordinary topics which people discuss when they first come together, and not finding the circle of their ideas enlarging, they fly asunder in search of that entertainment which each can no longer supply to the other. Here, then, the resources of a rural library would come into play, if the house were comfortable, and a good free library established in the neighbourhood.

Among the Orientals, the lower classes, who, like our own, can seldom read, have recourse for amusement to those living libraries, the storytellers. These individuals, whether men or women, are not mere narrators of fiction. They read the poets as well as the historians and philosophers, and interlard their narratives with apt quotations, moral maxims, anecdotes, and illustrations of manners. To hear them, the poor Arab, who has no books at home, and if he had, would be unable to read them, goes to the humble coffee-house, with twenty, thirty, or forty of his countrymen, to be delighted by the marvellous adventures described by the storyteller.

In these compositions, the authors address themselves too much perhaps to the imaginations of their hearers; but occasionally they enter into details which our novel readers might consider very tedious. For example, in order to impart additional interest to their marvellous incidents and wild exploits, they delineate to the best of their abilities the countries in which they are supposed to take place. Thus a peasant of the Upper Nile, is instructed in the geography of Ceylon, learns the existence of cannibalism in the Andaman islands, or hears of the combats between the elephant and the rhinoceros among the vast forests of Cape Unsang, and is enlightened about those delicate birds' nests which, in the further East, sell for their weight in gold, to be melted into soup for the gratification of Asiatic epicureans.

Persons who acquire the knowledge they possess in this way, have often wonderful memories. Being unable to commit anything to writing, they bestow on what they hear a degree of attention scarcely ever witnessed in these northern countries. I have known an Arab peasant who could keep in his head an exact account of all that, during a journey, had been laid out in a week, though many articles were purchased with coins not exceeding the fortieth part of two-pence-halfpenny in value. I tried him by putting down everything myself, and found his account to tally with my written one, even to a mite. These facts by no means diminish our respect for the letters of the alphabet, though they show how much an ingenious people can effect without them.

But neither books, nor conversation, nor anything else will ever reconcile a man to an uncomfortable home, to a slovenly wife and dirty children. The most must be made of the resources of the family; there must be contentment and cheerfulness, things irreconcilable with sordid habits and an ill-conditioned habitation.

In many parts of the world, the women possess more knowledge than the men, as well as a superior talent for management. This was the case among the old Egyptians; it is the case among the modern French. Even in Paris, the women of the humble classes carry on nearly all the business that is carried on. They write better, keep accounts better, exhibit greater adroitness in selling and buying, converse more fluently and sensibly, and generally appear to belong to an order of society above that of their husbands. This, however, does not at all proceed from their possessing more natural intelligence, but from their having cultivated their faculties more carefully.

Among us, women have never had fair play. Our ladies, taken altogether, are the most intelligent in the world, and yet they are far from being the most conversible. They have a notion that this or that department of knowledge—politics and theology for example—are not suited to their sex, and they accordingly eschew all discussions arising out of them.

It is extremely difficult, however, to determine how we ought to proceed in imparting knowledge to women. An old philosopher has observed, that where women are left uneducated, the nation can be but half happy. It may be questioned whether it can be happy at all. And yet, how are they to be instructed,

I mean among the industrious classes? It would be far better to leave women in a state of absolute ignorance, than, by our manner of teaching them, to take away any of their feminine qualities. A woman's education should be as feminine as her sex. Knowledge, when left to take its own course, and when delivered as it should be, assumes a womanly character in passing into the female mind. Regarded in the abstract, it is like metal in fusion, with which the sculptor may cast a Hercules or an Artemis. Everything in this case depends upon the tendency of the system we adopt.

CHAPTER XI.

IMPORTANCE OF FEMALE EDUCATION.

Institutes for Women.—Lectures.—Itinerant Lecturers.—Opinions of Noblemen.—Aristocratic Instructors.—Their Advantages.—Proper Teachers of Women.—Defective Education.—Fondness of Women for Oral Instruction.—False Ideas of Women.—Necessity of Educating them.—Influence of Mothers on their Children.—Debasing Effects of Poverty.—Working Women's Colleges.—Well and Ill-ordered Cottages.—The Mother's Precepts.—Influence of the Hearth.—Division of Time,—Recreation and Rest.—Female Incentives to Duty.—Paramount Importance of Women's Education.

SOME persons, anxious to promote the education of women, maintain that both sexes should study together at mechanics' institutes. They appear to believe that this would be the way to excite emulation and augment the appetite for knowledge. Their theory, however, in my opinion, is altogether wrong. To bring young men and women together under such circumstances, would hardly lead to the prosecution of serious studies. There would inevitably be trifling and unprofitable talk, calculated to hurry away the mind from the pursuit of knowledge. The Rev. Mr. Maurice, founder and principal of the Working Men's College in Great Ormond-street, takes precisely the same view. He says, "Very soon after the foundation of the Working Men's College, some of our teachers became anxious to make it available also for the instruction of women. Our pupils very cordially responded to the proposition, and would have been quite willing that the women should have been instructed, if we had thought fit, in the same classes with themselves. This plan, after careful consideration, we determined not to attempt. It seemed more wise to engage the services of ladies in the work, still connecting it as far as possible with our own."

Wherever means will permit, institutions should be formed exclusively for the use of women, with suitable libraries and helps to intellectual improvement. Among these must be reckoned lectures on various subjects, though many are apt to overrate the importance of this form of instruction.

By himself, the lecturer can do very little, save that, now and then, perhaps, he may create in the minds of his hearers a thirst for knowledge. The lecturer dresses up his materials, often scraped together for the occasion, unexamined and ill-digested, into a form calculated to administer amusement and excite laughter, things harmless enough in themselves, but not much in harmony with investigations into the planetary system or the structure of the earth, or the laws which regulate the movements of organized or unorganized matter.

The lecturer can rarely adapt his reasonings and illustrations to the mental calibre of his audience. He has his discourse cut and dried, and his illustrations to match, and goes about from town to town, reciting the self-same composition to all kinds of hearers. Sometimes, by chance, what he says may be suited, and therefore profitable, to his auditors; but in nine cases out of ten, or perhaps still more frequently, his arguments, anecdotes, metaphors, and similes, fall upon stony ground, and strike no root.

Several noblemen take a still more unfavourable view of professional lecturers, who, according to them, fill the minds of their hearers with mischievous ideas; under which term they may possibly intend to point out erroneous opinions in religion or politics, false or inadequate judgments of great authors, or lax systems of morality, calculated to sap and undermine the social edifice.

To supply popular audiences with superior mental food, these persons have begun to cultivate the habit of delivering lectures themselves. As, for example, Lord John Russell, Lord Stanley, the Duke of Newcastle, Lord Robert Cecil, Sir John Pakington, Sir Thomas Page Wood, the Bishops of Manchester, Salisbury, and Winchester, Sir James Kaye Shuttleworth, and Sir Robert Peel.

These gentlemen, when they undertake to impart knowledge to the people, possess many advantages over the persons who convert lecturing into a trade. They are under no necessity of speaking on subjects which they do not understand; they can bestow what time they please on the discourses they intend to deliver; they have received the best education the country can supply, and been rendered by experience familiar with the working of our institutions. It is certain, also, that a perpetual sense of independence, familiarity with great subjects, and the conversation, if they desire it, of intellectual men, must inspire them with liberal opinions and generous sentiments.

Consequently, should their voluntary performances fall short of our expectations, we ought not to indulge in severity of censure. Here, therefore, the will, in part at least, should be taken for the deed.

But the people will need a different order of teachers, teachers more skilful in the art of imparting instruction, who have mingled with the humbler classes, and by careful observation discovered their wants, and the best means of supplying them. It is above all things difficult to adapt oral teaching to the necessities of women. Their primary education is generally so defective, they are so little accustomed in youth to employ the faculties of their minds, and so afraid of profiting by the riches of conversation, that they too often continue all their lives intellectually in the condition of children. To address persons thus circumstanced, I mean so as to enable them to benefit by what they hear, is no easy task, and therefore it can occasion us no surprise that, of all the distinguished individuals above mentioned, scarcely one has put his information into the shape best fitted to enlighten the minds of women.

Still, lectures may be of service under certain circumstances, that is, when written and delivered by men of real ability, and who, among their other qualifications, possess a thorough knowledge of those whom they address.

Women generally are partial to lectures chiefly when they are rendered entertaining. This fact, therefore, should be kept in view by all who undertake to allure the female mind into the domains of knowledge.

Philosophers themselves, with all their researches into human nature, sometimes shoot wide of the mark, when treating of the idiosyncrasies of the female character. As a rule, their estimate of it is too low. Because women differ from men quite as much in their intellectual powers as in their material organization, we are not to conclude them to be inferior. No doubt they are unfitted by nature for some kinds of mental toil, but, on the other hand, they excel pre-eminently in others; and therefore, in the management of their education, we should be careful always to bear in mind what nature designed them to accomplish, and not run counter to her dictates.

At all events women must be educated, or men never will be properly. Women are as much the mothers of their children's minds as of their bodies, and, when duly qualified, impart nutriment to both with the same bounty.

When the soul first looks abroad upon the world, it is of infinite importance upon what sort of countenances it gazes,—whether they be loving and intelligent, full of tenderness and piety, or stolid, sordid, coarse, ignorant, and unsympathising.

It is true that nearly all mothers abound with love, and would benefit their children if they could. But when they are ignorant, when their ideas are vulgar, when their manners are coarse, when their souls are unilluminated by piety, what can they do towards modelling, purifying, and strengthening the infant souls intrusted to their care? It is a fact universally known, that nearly all great men have had great women for their mothers. The training and disciplining of man begins from the cradle, from the first maternal embrace; and it is of the greatest import what kind of ideas the mind first receives into itself.

Poverty is chiefly mischievous, where women are concerned, in reference to the associations it necessitates, the habits to which it gives rise, the ignorance it fosters, the feelings of despondency, distrust, doubt, and often self-contempt which it begets in the mind. Whatever consequently tends to improve the condition of the industrious classes, must tend necessarily at the same time to better their understandings. This may be done by the aid of those institutions which are now rapidly springing up all over the land, but as yet without sufficient regard being had to the improvement of women. A beginning may be said to have been made by the establishment of the Working Women's College, in Great Ormond-street, which owes its existence to the benevolent exertions of the Rev. Mr. Maurice. The ideas on which this institution is based are generally in harmony with the true theory of female education. The author of a Report on the State of the College gives a concise but interesting account of its esta-

blishment. " If ladies," he says, " could be found to
commence classes for working women in a house
already devoted to the purposes of a college, it
seemed not altogether improbable that they might
themselves in time become portions of a college,
which should bring different classes more into fellowship with each other, which should educate ladies
for occupations wherein they could be helpful to the
less fortunate members of their own sex, and wherein
they might benefit by hints received from ours."

In furtherance of this design, several medical men,
lawyers, and clergymen, delivered lectures on practical subjects, and a number of those ladies who took
an interest in the institution.   Experience can alone
show the result of any course of study ; but it appears
to me that some of the subjects insisted on in the
Working Women's College are scarcely suited to the
students,—for example, physiology and medicine. The
other branches of study appear to be well chosen :—
reading and writing, arithmetic, history, geography,
natural history, vocal music, drawing, needlework,
Bible-class lectures, duties to each other, readings in
Shakespeare.   The classes are held from three to five
in the afternoon, partly that they may not interfere
with the lessons to the working men, partly because
that time is more convenient to the teachers than

the evening would be.   It was feared that these
hours might be inconvenient to the women themselves ; but it has been found that many have overcome all the difficulties which seemed to lie in the
way of their studies, and that the number of students
is constantly on the increase.   The Report concludes
with the following remark :—" The subjects are of
a more elementary kind than some of those in our
general programme ; for the knowledge of females in
the working classes is generally below that of their
husbands and brothers."

They who have examined the state of education
in Scotland make the same observation.   It appears
upon the whole, that the mental condition of the
industrious classes in that country is rather dete-
riorating than otherwise.   This may in part be owing
to the inadequate stipends paid to the parochial
schoolmasters, though it may also be feared that
something is to be set down to the lower estimation
in which the poor are held by the upper orders.
Formerly it was not very uncommon to find in
Scotland, even among the humbler classes, women
who could read Latin ; and, though this may be very
compatible with much ignorance on familiar and
useful things, it implied at least that some attention
had been paid to their bringing up.   At present,

even in the most civilized counties, the women of Scotland, though naturally among the most intelligent in the world, are deplorably ignorant, slovenly in their persons, and disorderly in their households.

When women are well instructed, look at the difference it makes in the household ! Contrast a modest, intelligent, industrious mother, with one who is careless, slovenly, unmindful of what is due to herself and to her family. In one case the hearth, however humble, is brooded over by a moral beauty not to be witnessed without delight ; and in the other we behold nothing but discontent, discord, squalor, and misery. When mothers are what they should be, the children, with such exceptions as we must always look for in this world, will be affectionate, laborious, and full of enterprise ; the mother's sayings are converted into maxims, which often regulate, like the laws of the Medes and Persians, the conduct of both boys and girls when they grow up to be men and women, aye, and to be old men and women too, when the lips which delivered those sayings have long perhaps been silent in the dust. The wisest, and boldest, and bravest man often does not know how much of his success in life, of the powers he has developed, of the honours and distinction he has won, may be traced to the scenes he witnessed, and the conversations he heard, by his father's fireside.

Our first effort, therefore, should be to impart proper instruction to the women of the people, to elevate their understandings, to regulate their habits, to exalt and purify their minds.

In pursuing this plan, however, we must not lose sight of the truth, that the life of all classes, to be healthful and profitable, must be divided into three parts, one devoted to labour, one to study, and one to recreation and rest. The opulent will not pretend that they devote all their leisure to the acquisition of knowledge, and that when their business (for all people have business) is over, they rush like wolves to study. If they did, they would be very absurd. Knowledge is only valuable in so far as it teaches us how to live; but if we spend all our time in acquiring it, we do not live at all. We are mere machines or receptacles of ideas, not breathing active intelligences, with innumerable duties to perform, and willing and able to perform them.

Consider the multiplied relations of a man in this world, as a son, as a husband, as a father, as a friend, as a citizen, as a Christian; duties attach to him in each and all, and it is in order to perform them properly that he studies. Women's duties are peculiar, obscure, almost unknown. Men have the voice of fame, the opinion of the world, the approbation of

their companions, to urge them on ; women, for the
most part, have nothing but the smile of their husbands or of their families.   Sometimes they have not
even this, and are obliged to derive all the consola-
tion they have from the consciousness of having
performed their duties faithfully.   I repeat, then, that
in accomplishing the great reformation which is now
expected to be brought about by Schools, Lyceums,
and Institutes, the greatest possible importance should
be attached to the training, disciplining, and education
of women, without which the whole scheme will inevitably prove abortive.

The Duke of Newcastle, in words which imply a
refined sympathy with his poorer countrywomen, expresses the same conviction.   " He referred to the advantages to be derived from Lending-Libraries, which
must carry knowledge to the mothers of families, and
thus elevate and sanctify the whole household.   It is
very certain that the education of the people ought
to begin with that of women, which is to be effected
rather by books than by lectures or classes.   Women
cannot frequent reading-rooms, but must have the
books at home, that they may take them up when
they happen to have spare time.   Cheap books, therefore, are of great service, though not when they are
printed with small type, and in lines huddled so closely

together that the unpractised eye can scarcely distinguish one from another."

Even in our Asiatic provinces, before the breaking out of the troubles, a desire had sprung up among the Natives to extend the blessings of education to women. Gopal Singh, a Hindú gentleman holding under Government the post of district inspector of native schools, had succeeded, through his own exertions, in establishing upwards of two hundred seminaries for young ladies in the province of Agra, which were attended by three thousand eight hundred girls of the best families. By many of our countrymen in India this is regarded rather as a social revolution than as an educational movement. As a rule, the Natives look with suspicion on everything which comes from a foreigner, for which reason the great efforts made by the English have not produced corresponding results. I copy, almost *verbatim*, from the ' Friend of India,' the history of this system of schools, which is partly given in Gopal Singh's own words. " The establishment of a little school," observes the Pundit, " in which my own daughters, and those of my immediate friends and relations attended, at first, like a charm, dispelled in a great measure the prejudices of my neighbours, and induced many to send their girls also. This example, and my constant persuasion and reasoning, have at last succeeded in inducing many respectable inhabitants of other villages to yield." And so the movement bids fair to become national. The pupils are nearly all Hindús, belonging to the more respectable classes. The teachers are all men. " Want of female teachers," says Gopal Singh, " was one great obstacle in the way; but the guardians of the girls, composing the respective schools, pointed out men of approved character, in whom they have full confidence, and I have appointed such persons only as teachers; the result is very satisfactory." Only in the city of Agra, where the wealthy bankers and merchants have been persuaded to establish a girls' school, has any objection been made to male instructors. But Agra will soon be abundantly supplied with teachers from among the more advanced pupils of the rural schools. Lieutenant Fuller, the Inspector of Schools, reports that about one-tenth of the whole number of pupils are more than twenty years of age, the remainder varying from six to twenty years. The ' Delhi Gazette,' in noticing these remarkable facts, suggests that " Pundit Gopal should be at once relieved from all other duties, and enabled to devote himself entirely to a work for which he has shown such peculiar aptitude. The suggestion is a good one. The Pundit should receive a

liberal salary, and should be left utterly free from
the usual restraints. Too much interference, even too
much patronage, on the part of English officials,
might spoil all. The Pundit has evidently struck a
vein of native feeling, which he must be allowed to
pursue in his own way."

In Calcutta still greater progress has been made,
though in a different direction. The Hindú gentlemen
educated at the English Colleges often bring their
wives and daughters to hear the lectures of professors.
Of course these ladies have been taught English, and
accustomed to read English books. When they adopt
Christianity, and go into society, they soon speak
English fluently, and give proof of much intelligence
and vigour of mind. There, however, as in Agra, the
development of the educational system is checked by
the insuperable objection of the Natives to have their
ladies taught by men. These objections, I think, are
well founded; and Professor Maurice, in establishing
the Working Women's College in London, recognized
their full force. The American missionary, Hill,
had to encounter similar obstacles in his attempt to
impart instruction to the women of Greece; and it
was not until his wife generously undertook the female department that any success was obtained. In
fact, it is better that women should remain ignorant,
than that they should be systematically taught by men.

CHAPTER XII.

BOOKS FOR THE PEOPLE.

THE conviction is fast spreading, that, to create an
intelligent people, books must be used as the chief
instrument. Some, however, who affect to be philosophical over-much, maintain that what they denominate " book knowledge " is scarcely necessary to
qualify individuals for excelling in works of industry.

But there is no kind of labour which can be done without the aid of the mind. Whatever, therefore, improves and strengthens the mind, must fit its possessor to display superiority in industry.

Take, for example, household affairs. It is certain that a woman well instructed, with refined tastes and habits,—which a woman may have, even in the humblest station,—will manage the concerns of her family, and provide for them, much better than one whose intelligence has never been awakened.

It strengthens our hopes for the success of education, to observe that gentlemen of rank and influence are beginning, not only to admit the practicability of instructing the people, but contending for its desireableness, and contributing to hasten its diffusion. The truths upon which they insist may be perfectly well known to those who read and reflect. But this is no objection to their being dwelt upon. It is in fact a capital error to be constantly searching in matters like these for rare thoughts and recondite discoveries. No man should be ashamed to repeat again and again an useful observation or maxim which, though perfectly well known to the learned, may be by no means familiar to the majority of mankind.

Besides we must not disguise from ourselves the fact, that a very large number of persons think much less of what is said, than of who has said it. Aware of this, the Duke of Newcastle, in his Address to the inhabitants of Retford, seeks to recommend an unquestionable truth by connecting it with a celebrated name. He refers to the saying of Napoleon Buonaparte, that much of the future conduct of a man depends greatly upon his mother. If this be true, and there can be no doubt of it, Lending Libraries must be of the greatest utility; for in affording instruction and good advice to a mother, they are imparting it to a whole family. His Grace then concludes by remarking that he thought it necessary to dilate at some length upon the benefits to be derived from reading useful works, which could not fail to make men, good men, good husbands, and good Christians; " it tends to civilize and Christianize all those around the domestic hearth, and will not tend to sap, but to encourage, religious knowledge, without which all our other knowledge is but as dross."

From this observation, the transition is natural to book-hawking. This plan of awakening the minds of the humbler classes originated during the eighteenth century in France. It is true that the object proposed by its inventors, differed altogether from that which is aimed at by the friends of education in this country. But though the design was in some respects blamable, the mode of fulfilling it exhibited extraordinary ingenuity.

A Publication Committee was established at Paris, which selected and printed the works intended to be circulated, partly by private presses, partly by those of Switzerland, Germany, and Holland. When ready for sale, usually at the cheap price of five pence, they were delivered to the hawkers, who were allowed a large profit. These men, directed by the agents of the Committee, diffused the books over the whole kingdom, until scarcely a village or hamlet in France remained unimbued with the new opinions.

We propose to ourselves in this country no such object.* Our wish is to call forth the mental powers of the people, in order thereby to promote their best interests. Almost from time immemorial the book-hawking system has been in operation, under two very different influences.

The Religious Societies scatter their publications far and wide among the humbler classes, but there are other divisions of the poor who, not having anything better to read, waste their time on worthless

* At present book-hawkers, like all other hawkers, require a license. Mr. Davis, Secretary to the Religious Tract Society, proposes to do away with this license, when the books sold by the hawker are religious. The shortest and best way, however, is to abolish it altogether.

and criminal publications. Dying speeches have a
great charm for them; they buy them by millions,
and thus introduce mischievous ideas into their minds,
there to ferment, and prepare them for the com-
mission of crime. Depraved prints and handbills
also circulate largely among the working-classes, together with cheap blasphemous books, which tend at
once to destroy their religion and their morals. It
is said that, of this class, nearly thirty millions are
circulated annually, which is almost equal to the
issues of all the Religious Societies put together.

But, supposing the pious productions to be far
greater in number, would it be safe to infer that their
influence is greater in proportion? The tracts, sermons, and so on, are generally given away, and not
unfrequently to people unable to profit by them.

Walking one day through a green lane in Somerset-
shire, I noticed a boy employed to watch a cow,
seated amid wild flowers on the grass, with a number
of tracts before him. I inquired if he had read them,
and he replied that he could not read. When I further asked what he did with them, he pointed to two
gentlemen, a short distance before me, who he said
had thrown them to him as they passed. He added
that I might have them if I liked, as they were of no
use to him.

The immoral publications are not thus distributed. On the contrary, they are paid for with money, and are eagerly sought after, not only by the rising generations, but by the generations which have already risen. How is this evil to be remedied? There is, in my opinion, no means but one; and that is, putting better books within the reach of the people.

A new trade has sprung up, probably in consequence of the multiplication of cheap books. This is one of the most important steps that have been taken towards diffusing knowledge among the people. While books continued dear, and were only to be had in fine shops, the people would not think of them. To buy exceeded their means; and even if it had not, they would have been restrained, by the consciousness of their own rough and humble appearance, from entering those elegant shops in which they would have expected to meet the opulent grandees of the neighbourhood.

But now, when the hawker comes to their cottages, they experience no repugnance to talk with him, to examine his stock, to listen to his recommendations, to learn from him what new books have lately appeared, and what are expected. He belongs to their own order, he dresses like them, talks like them, a little more knowingly perhaps, but still in their dialect.

On the character of the books thus circulated, it is necessary to make some remarks. It is only a particular class of the poor who care for tracts, or for strictly religious books. Works of general literature of an interesting and useful nature, might be added with good effect to the hawker's stock, because in this way the number of buyers would be increased, and the appetite of the people for valuable knowledge greatly stimulated. Works connected with our own history, popular poetry, and lively books of travels, and even good novels, might be made to co-operate in awakening and correcting the popular taste.

Nearly all the old books intended for the use of the humbler classes have a mean and poverty-stricken aspect, as if they would proclaim the fact that knowledge, in passing down to the poor, should throw off its gorgeous robes, its brightness and its beauty, and look bald and naked, or be clad in tatters like themselves; it is time to banish such works from the people's library. Nothing more is needed in popular literature, than that it should be written in good idiomatic English, free from pedantry, from affectation, from scraps of foreign languages, from allusions to the more obscure facts of science. It is remarkable that literature generally improves in proportion to the largeness of the field it has to fertilize.

When men wrote for the few, they wrote in Latin, or interlarded their English with quotations from the learned languages, which rendered their style caviare to the general. When books began to find more readers, English not only superseded Latin, but the style was more carefully attended to, words were arranged with greater reference to the natural order, punctuation was studied, the length of sentences was diminished, everything, in short, was done to ensure clearness.

We must now be on our guard against the lowering of the style of literature, which many persons suppose to be needed in writing for the people. Our aim ought not to be to disennoble literature, but to elevate the popular mind.

What, however, are the books which at present find most favour with the people? One of them, at least, reasoning *à priori*, we should certainly never have expected to find popular. However, experience shows us the loftiest poetical creation of modern times, making its way into the humblest cottages, side by side with ' Robinson Crusoe ' and ' The Pilgrim's Progress,'—I mean, ' Paradise Lost.' How are we to account for this? By reflecting upon the character of the poem, profoundly religious, and pervaded throughout by those grand and heroic sentiments, which appeal, in all countries, to the great body of mankind, when left free to follow the bent of their own minds.

In connection with this poem, an amusing anecdote is told. Some honest son of toil, going into the library of a Mechanics' Institute, in search of a little amusement after a day's labour, asked for ' Jack Sheppard.' " It is out," replied the librarian. " Oh, then," said the hungerer after excitement, " bring me ' Paradise Lost.' " If he could not get the adventures of thieves and profligates, he would feast his imagination with pictures of perfect innocence, and of the land where celestial rivers

"Roll o'er Elysian flowers their amber streams."

But it appears, from the testimony of those who have most carefully examined the subject, that our literature does not supply a sufficient number of books calculated, at the same time, to hit the taste of the people, and to enlarge and purify their minds; and various suggestions have been thrown out, on the means of supplying this deficiency. Some have recommended one class of books, and some another. One very ingenious gentleman suggests that a series of local histories would be likely to prove beneficial. But it may well be questioned whether the great body of the people are ever likely to acquire a taste for parochial antiquities, or, if they did, whether they would benefit much by such a study.

The truth is, the people never take to books manufactured exclusively for them. . No one has yet been able to discover what it is that makes a book popular. Men of very great genius have failed in their attempts to create one, while persons of inferior abilities have now and then succeeded. But it is with books as with men,—they are the most popular who most resemble the people in the make and colour of their minds, while they possess besides, a greater fund of knowledge, and a vivacious and genial manner of communicating their ideas.

At any rate, no one can say beforehand, how a man or a book will be received by the world. It appears necessary, in all cases, to be swayed openly or secretly by the wish to please; this almost always begets a certain amount of goodwill: but in order to obtain any great success, there must be, over and above, a vivacity, a warmth, and a power of suggesting new trains of thought. The people, and women especially, are not to be allured into the field of knowledge by the mere motive of utility. What is useful, is not always pleasant, neither is what is pleasant, always useful. It is only a well disciplined mind that will consent to take bitters to augment its strength.

There must be a fascination in literature, and it must not only give delight from the outset, but abound in promises of perpetual enjoyment. For this reason, biographies, real or fictitious, are almost sure, if well written, to command popular favour. Voltaire's ' Life of Charles XII. of Sweden,' is known to hundreds of thousands, who have never read his tragedies, his Letters, or his Essay on General History.

Again, even boys read Tacitus's ' Life of Agricola ;' and Plutarch, throughout Europe, has always been the most popular of ancient writers. Why? Obviously because his narratives, escaping from the generalities of history, carry the reader into the more agreeable walks of private life. David Hume tells an amusing anecdote about the effect of these Lives upon a woman of fashion. " I remember," he says, " that I was once desired by a young beauty, for whom I had some passion, to send her some novels and romances for her amusement in the country, but was not so ungenerous as to take the advantage which such a course of reading might have given me, being resolved not to make use of poisoned arms against her. I therefore sent her Plutarch's Lives, assuring her, at the same time, that there was not a word of truth in them, from beginning to end. She perused them very attentively till she

came to the lives of Alexander and Cæsar, whose
names she had heard of by accident, and then returned me the books, with many reproaches for deceiving her."

Dr. Johnson used to say, that no man's life, if
properly written, would prove uninteresting. This is
true, but the difficulty is to write properly, biography, or anything else. However, the lives of
remarkable men, when faithfully related, even without
any extraordinary degree of ability, are always instructive, and often become widely popular. Thus
the life of Johnson himself, though written by a man
of very moderate talents, garrulous, gossiping, and
inflated with vanity, is yet one of the most fascinating
books in our language, because the biographer was
thoroughly possessed by his subject, and converted
himself into a sort of echo, by which the sayings of
the peremptory, but most kind and amiable Doctor,
were repeated for the benefit of posterity.

In our contemporary literature, there are several
biographies which ought to be introduced into the
people's library. All these I should like to enu-
merate, but I must content myself with mentioning
Mr. Forster's life of Goldsmith; Mr. Dixon's lives
of Howard, Penn, and Blake; Mr. Bayle St. John's
life of Montaigne; Mr. Morley's lives of Palissy the

Potter and Girolamo Cardano; and Mr. Roscoe's life of Cervantes.

It is still more pleasant, when men and women become their own historians, and relate honestly their experiences of life. That they will apologize for their own failings is natural, and therefore to be expected. But some men, like Montaigne, Rousseau, and even Bunyan, delight in exaggerating their faults, partly that they may appear to have outlived them, and to have become sufficiently wise and impartial to sit in judgment upon themselves; partly by way of atoning for what they have done amiss; but chiefly, perhaps, in order to display their own ingenuity and eloquence, and to ingratiate themselves with mankind, who love to contemplate the example of men distinguished quite as much, perhaps, for their frailties and shortcomings, as for their genius, their learning, or their virtue.

Here then is a class of works, which, with a few exceptions, may be profitably diffused among the people. Fictitious narratives are only powerful inasmuch as they resemble truth, and therefore cannot possess equal fascination with truth itself. We say of the former, that the events they describe might have happened; but of the latter, that they have happened. There is a double interest, the interest of the facts, and the interest excited by beholding an individual studying the circumstances of his own career, and making himself the hero of his own epic. The reading of such works is well calculated to call forth all the powers of reflection. As he studies his parents, his schoolfellows, his friends, and shows how their qualities and affections acted upon him for good or for evil, so the reader is incited to look about him, and examine and consider the character of those who, by their authority or proximity, influence his own conduct or thoughts.

Every man is to himself what Plato calls the Great Year. He has his sowing time and his growing time, his weeding, his irrigating, and his harvest. The principles and ideas he puts into his mind in youth, lie there, it may be, for many years, apparently unprolific. But nothing dies. There is a process going on unseen, and by the touch of circumstances, the man springs forth into strength, he knows not how, as if by miracle. But after all, he only reaps as he had sown.

Reading, wild, desultory, and often to all appearance idle, leaves nevertheless behind it something good or bad in the memory. If the intellect be powerful, there comes a time when it feels itself under he necessity of reviewing its stores, and drawing upon them for use. Then, if the previous life has been misspent, is the season for regret, when one compartment after another of the mind is opened, and found to contain nothing useful. The man finds himself exposed, naked or badly armed, to the fierce assaults of circumstances, and perhaps falls almost unpitied in the struggle.

But biographers generally describe a successful contest. The man who has achieved nothing, has scarcely the courage to depict a blank and barren existence. If he thinks of it, he soon recoils from the task, and consents, not without many pangs, to pass away into forgetfulness. The man who dares to write his own life, believes at least that he has done something worthy to be remembered, either as a warning, or as an example. The chief drawback of biography is this, that few lives keep the promise of their beginning. No matter whether the soul rises in splendour or under a cloud, the dawning of life is always bright and beautiful. Poverty, misfortune, the want of friends, nothing can entirely overcast the light which accompanies the morning of existence. As it advances, errors, indolence, false steps, rashness, impede the march of the mind. Intellect is subjugated by passion, and long years are perhaps required to repair the mistake of a moment.

Sometimes men are not sufficiently conscious of the wants and tastes of the age in which they live, and labour for forms of society passed away or unborn. Their creations do not speak to their contemporaries, and they fall, therefore, of necessity into the background, and often go out of life unnoticed.

Still the picture of their career is highly instructive, since it is quite as necessary to know what to shun, as what to follow. Besides, there are men whose happiness does not consist in attracting the attention of others. They think, and live, and labour, whether in literature or in art, merely because they experience delight in exercising the powers of their minds. The fountain of their joy is in themselves. If others seek to share it, they are welcome, but their approval forms no part of the happiness of these worshippers of the Muses. The ancient poet who lived and died on a desert island, without pen, ink, and paper, was not therefore miserable. His visions were always with him, investing all his hours with splendour, and at last closed his eyes like so many ministering angels.

It must do good to the artisan and the labourer to have their humble dwellings lighted up by revelations of the life of genius; and in many cases, when the seed falls on good ground, they will be inspired to go and do likewise. No one knows where the intellectual element is to be found, until it bursts forth. Whole generations have walked over beds of gold, ay, even when it glittered amid the dust beneath their feet, without once suspecting the existence of those hidden treasures. It is the same with our humble classes. What beauty, what greatness, what piety, what virtue, lie latent in their souls, we know not, and shall never know unless we apply ourselves diligently to remove the heavy masses of ignorance which now completely overlay them.

CHAPTER XIII.

EDUCATIONAL RATE.

Attempting too much.—Various forms of Study.—Sir John Pakington.—Reasons for a Rate.—Napoleon's Scheme of Education.—Its
Military Character and Fatal Effects.—English System of Education. — Vast Resources of England. — Costliness of Ignorance.—
Machinery of Justice.—Education Cheaper than a Police.—Economy of a Rate.—Charity Schools.—Right to Education.—The
Feeling of Independence. — The Men who fought at Cressy and
Agincourt.—Tendency of Civilization.—Courage and Self-dependence.

IT is a proverbial failing of nearly all those who speak
or write on the subject of Education, to recommend
too much, to aim at impracticable things, and to
speculate upon the faculties of children and youths,
as if they were actually without limit. I may perhaps appear to have fallen into the same error. But,
in mapping out the world of study, I by no means
intend to maintain that everybody should do everything. I only say, here are certain things which may
be done, some by one class of persons, some by another. As all men, during their lives, stand in need

of the fruits of study, it is obvious that all should study more or less.

But how, in this country, are all to study. None but the wealthy can bestow on their children a good education, and they who belong to this class are far from numerous. Sir John Pakington, who deserves so much of the friends of knowledge, observes, in a speech delivered at Manchester, " that very few consider how immense is the numerical proportion of our fellow-countrymen who are interested in the question of national education. Out of a population of eighteen millions, in England and Wales, there are only about four hundred and eighty thousand, who derive, from any source, a yearly income of a hundred or more. Taking the numbers at half a million, and allowing five persons to a family, there will remain fifteen millions and a half, of men, women, and children, who are dependent upon incomes of less than a hundred a year." He then adds, " that every man whose means are less than a hundred a year, must look to a cheap and good education for his children, as among, not the secondary, but the primary necessaries of life. The question is not then limited merely to labouring men. The tradesman and the farmer, as a rule, in matters of education, pay dearly for a bad article; and if every existing school in England were

what it ought to be, instead of being exactly the reverse, there would be, in every town and village, schools
in which the children of the labourer might receive the
blessings of elementary instruction."

We might almost infer from this passage, that
schools are already sufficiently numerous, though of
inferior quality. But Sir John Pakington is not, in
reality, of this opinion. He feels, as much as any
one, the necessity of establishing new schools as well
as of improving the methods of instruction in such
as already exist. To accomplish this purpose, however, it seems absolutely necessary to have recourse
to an Educational Rate. Against this plan there are
many objections, the principal of which is, that it
would throw too much power into the hands of the
Government, and enable it to impress what character
it pleased, upon the intelligence of the country. We
have witnessed, in a neighbouring State, the results
of a system like that towards which, in the opinion of
many, the tendencies of the age are hurrying us.

When Napoleon Buonaparte rose to supreme power
in France, he made use of the machinery created by
the Republic, to discipline and indoctrinate the French
people. Regarding it from his point of view, it
would be difficult to accord it too much admiration.
It created an educational hierarchy, the original and

central principle of which, under the name of University, resided in Paris, while the inferior establishments, multiplying as they descended in rank, spread over the whole empire. Had time permitted, this wonderful organization would have exerted its influence over the minds of all Frenchmen, and left no such thing as absolute ignorance in the country. The only defect of this system, lay in the spirit which pervaded it.

Napoleon, in his way, was a great student of antiquity, and took the hint of his organization from Lycurgus. He wished to convert the French into a nation of soldiers, and very nearly succeeded. Everything in his system was military. Both professors and students wore uniforms, and every idea transmitted from mind to mind, had the impress of the camp upon it. No institution could possibly be more hostile to civil liberty, to social improvement, or to the happiness of the domestic hearth; but the principles set at work in the Tuileries, penetrated through the whole body of the French nation, as with the rapidity of electric wires, and made every heart tremble at the beat of the drum : I mean, tremble with delight. All other feelings were submerged beneath that of glory, the glory which springs from trampling out freedom in neighbouring countries, from destroying harvests, from burning villages, and massacring their inhabitants, and from converting populous cities into ruinous heaps.

But such is the force of education, that, for more than a quarter of a century, the French people were completely reconciled to this callous and hardhearted system, which was rapidly changing French society into a machine for manufacturing sabres, and things, in the shape of men, to wield them, without the slightest reference to justice or injustice, to religion, refinement, or humanity. It will take whole ages to obliterate from the French soil, the traces of that tremendous system of education, favourable enough to the development of the physical sciences, but altogether destructive to morals, to patriotism, to liberty, and to genius.

Under Napoleon, there was no literature with a soul in it, and painting and sculpture degenerated into mere mechanical contrivances for giving *éclat* to devastation and bloodshed.

I merely allude to this system to show how much, for good or for evil, may be effected in a few years, by a carefully organized plan of instruction. We are not at all likely to imitate it, or the Prussian system, which has risen into estimation since the fall of Napoleon. Our education will be English, English in its form, English in the ideas conveyed, English in the object aimed at; but by considering what other nations with much less means have been able to achieve, we may be encouraged to put forth our power in order that what they did for despotism, we may do for that freedom which is the best and noblest birth-right of Englishmen.

When we reckon upon the resources of a nation, and that too the wealthiest and most powerful nation in the world, it is not easy to exaggerate what may be accomplished by making a proper use of those re-sources. It is only necessary to be convinced that, by dealing wisely with the rising generation, we may immensely diminish the cost of police establishments, of courts of justice, of prisons, hulks and penal set-tlements, to justify the expenditure, if necessary, of millions, in creating the moral habits and developing the mental faculties of the people.

Either knowledge and early discipline will affect the character of individuals, or they will not; if they will not, we may as well, or even better, leave the people as they are, but if they will affect them bene-ficially, then, exactly in proportion as they do so, must they diminish the necessity, and consequently the expense, of the apparatus of repression. If we lay out money in preventing crime, and succeed, it is obviously

quite as economical as laying out the same money afterwards in punishing crime. A schoolmaster perhaps
is as cheap as a policeman, and if well employed may
render the latter unnecessary. The question in fact
lies between the schoolhouse and the gaol, between
national schools and reformatories, between Lyceums
and Mechanics' Institutes, and Norfolk Island.

When any great moral good is to be effected, an
enlightened nation will not be deterred by considerations of expense, from putting forth whatever power
it possesses. Yet it is fortunate when economy and
morality are found to go hand in hand. The repression and punishment of crime, at present, absorb
in this country more than the revenues of a small
kingdom, falling very little short of four millions
sterling.

A large portion of this enormous expenditure is to
be set down to the account of our ignorance as a
community. Our state physicians have hitherto proved
themselves unequal either to cure or prevent the
disease. We pay therefore four millions sterling
as a tribute to the incapacity of our rulers; and it
begins at length to be suspected that, by expending
less than a moiety of that sum in disciplining and
instructing the people, we may not only save the
remainder, together with much that is now expended

in poor rates, but place the industrious classes in a condition to provide amply for themselves in future.

It is not therefore a mere question of economy. We must likewise take into account the pain, the sorrow, the suffering, the shame, the infamy, which thousands among the humbler classes would be spared.* This view of the matter must be pressed upon Parliament, which in the end will be convinced that a general rate, for the purpose of bringing education home to

---

* Sir John Pakington has frequently insisted on the great number of poor children who are suffered to run about the streets in every one of our cities. The ragged schools, established through the exertions of Lord Shaftesbury, have done much towards diminishing the evil; but the proportion of ignorant and vagrant children is still immense in Hereford, Manchester, Edinburgh, Bristol, and London. Our gaols are filled with recruits from this juvenile population, who have no parents, no home, and no one whatever to support them. They therefore live by begging, when they can; and when they can't, they steal. Their crime, however, is rather that of the country than their own. It would be absurd to expect that they should quietly lie down and die, when there is an abundance of food within their reach. In fact they have no choice but to steal; and their offences, which are involuntary, render necessary that vast and costly machinery of police, of courts of justice, reformatories, prisons, hulks, and penal settlements. It would obviously not be enough to establish schools for such children. They must be maintained, and taught trades so that they may be enabled to earn their own livelihood, otherwise these nomadic helots must inevitably become robbers, and subsist by making war upon property. When sufficiently instructed at the schools of emigration, hereafter to be described, they should be conveyed to the Colonies, where they would find what they could never obtain in this country, the means of honest independence.

every child's door, will be at once salutary and economical.

I do not affect to enter into details respecting the way in which such a rate should be levied—they who are acquainted with the mechanism of taxation will easily be able to determine that. I only desire to establish the principle that no impost would be more righteous in itself, or more cheerfully paid, than an education tax. Without it, we may no doubt accomplish much, and indeed much has already been accomplished; but the spread of knowledge will never equal the wants of the people until it is brought about by national means.

Lord John Russell, taking a statesmanlike view of the subject, contends that the rate ought to be general and compulsory, imposed by the Imperial Legislature, but entrusted, in the expenditure, to local management. But his views are far from being shared by a majority in Parliament. Even out-of-doors, perhaps, there exist considerable fear and misapprehension respecting the working and tendency of such a plan, which, in the opinion of many, might in the long-run prove destructive of civil liberty. No one, however, will imagine that Lord John Russell desires or contemplates such a result. He believes, and, I think, with reason, that, provided the Government leaves in the hands of the people themselves the form of instruction, and the nature of the knowledge imparted, no evil consequences need be apprehended.

This will put an end to charity schools, and deliver the people from the idea that they are educated as paupers. They will then have a right to education, because, in proportion to their means, they will pay for it. They will consequently approach the school in an erect posture, and not with hanging head and slouching gait, as if they were ashamed of the eleemosynary ideas they were going to receive. There is no feeling more valuable than the feeling of independence, which would be ill exchanged even for knowledge. An erudite pauper would be far inferior in dignity, valour, and the spirit of enterprise, to an independent savage, ready at any moment to risk his life in taking the scalp of his enemy.

Care therefore must be taken not to degrade while we instruct. Knowledge is good, but it is not everything in this world. Manly pride is also good; and it may be questioned whether the men who fell at Agincourt, Cressy, and Poictiers, were not, with all their ignorance, greatly superior in personal feeling to an equal number of the same class of men in the present day.

The tendency of civilization, if not checked by wise institutions, is to render men timid and effeminate. Our institutions, in many respects, are wise; and the conditions of society, which laws cannot regulate, exert of themselves a great power over our destiny.

It should be the aim of whatever system of instruction we adopt, and apply generally to the enlightening of the people, to foster habits of courage, hardihood, and self-dependence.

CHAPTER XIV.

AGRICULTURAL SCHOOLS.

Ignorance of the Peasantry.—Remark of Lord Robert Cecil.—Dean of Hereford's Schools.—Example of King's Somborne.—Education in Hampshire and Wiltshire.—The Half-time System.—Alternate Plough Boys.—Rural Tastes of the English.—Shakespeare the Homer of England.—Landscape Painters.—Beauty of English Scenery.—Science of Agriculture.—New Plants and Animals.—Dislike of Old Times unwise.—Ancient use of Guano.—Curious Reaping Machine.—Proper Studies of a Farmer.—Botany.—Natural History.—Chemistry.—The Fly.—Blight.—Children of the Peasants.—Burke.—Children's Time.—Lord Stanley.—Evening Studies.—Religion.—Morals.—History.—Politics.—Mingling of the Classes.—Switzerland and Germany.

To accomplish this purpose, we ought very greatly to multiply agricultural schools. Up to this time the name of peasant throughout Europe has been synonymous with ignorance. Placed in the midst of the grand operations of nature, and profoundly influenced by the vicissitudes of the seasons, he nevertheless remains in most countries almost as little conscious of the natural beauties around him as the team he drives, or the plough with which he breaks the furrows.

Struck by this fact, Lord Robert Cecil, in a speech delivered at Stamford, spoke of the stolidity of the English peasant as something indomitable. This was rather the effect of irritated enthusiasm than of hostility to the education of the poor. If applied to the whole race of agricultural labourers, his remark was wrong; but applying it to individuals, it is unfortunately too true.

To render the case otherwise with the rising generation, we ought to pursue and enlarge the plan which appears to have been first put in practice by the present Dean of Hereford, while he was rector of King's Somborne, in Hampshire. He conceived the idea that it would be practicable, by bringing together in the same schools the children of the farmer and the labourer, at once to create kindly feelings between the employers and the employed, and to impart to both a superior education. He made a commencement in his own parish; he overlooked the school, he went occasionally and taught in it himself; he laboured, and laboured successfully, to inspire the wealthy classes in the neighbourhood with a desire to co-operate in the diffusion of knowledge, and he now enjoys the satisfaction of beholding nearly eighty schools, in Hampshire and Wiltshire, which owe their existence entirely to the example he set at

King's Somborne, and to the exertions he made to enlighten his own neighbourhood.

In other parts of the country, similar efforts have been made to diffuse knowledge among the workers in iron, Miners, and Colliers. An association has been formed in the counties of Leicester, Nottingham, and Derby, by which the system of competitive examinations and prizes has been introduced. As might have been expected, however, there exist, both among the employers and the employed, persons who object to these schools as likely to impair the efficiency of the workmen. They persuade themselves that men, eager to possess scientific attainments, will be apt to cherish a distaste for what is practical. The experience of several parts of Europe should reassure them. In Hungary, Germany, and France, mining colleges and schools have long been established; and the effect of them has been, not to turn away the attention of workmen from the great business of their lives, but to render them more intelligent, skilful, and ambitious of excellence. At the Museum of Practical Geology in London, instruction is given in the higher branches of knowledge connected with mining; but in the ordinary schools, the attention of students should be strictly confined to such acquisitions as may be useful to them, and lie within their reach.

No error is more common than that of attempting too much; and into this, it appears to me, the mining colleges and schools of the Continent have in nearly all cases been betrayed. It is to be hoped that the superior good sense of our countrymen will enable them to steer clear of this mistake, which would prove fatal to the whole scheme. Teachers and professors, who have to deal exclusively with the theory of knowledge, are apt to forget the circumstances of workmen, and to imagine that, in the limited time at their disposal, they may learn everything. It is better to begin with a narrow circle of studies, including nothing but what is strictly useful. Afterwards, if it be found practicable, things agreeable and ornamental may be added; but these should be left to individual taste and inclination.

Out of the same influence arose " The Hants and Wilts Adult Education Society," which, notwithstanding its formidable name, is doing good service to the cause of knowledge. It has introduced the plan of competitive examinations in the history and theory of the steam-engine, the physical geography of the British Islands, and the history of England. This is an extension of the system adopted by Government and the East India Company, which has brought to light an incredible amount of ignorance among the middle classes. Mr. John Stuart Mill observes, that, from 1851 to 1854 inclusive, four hundred and thirty-seven gentlemen were examined for commissions in the Indian army; out of this number a hundred and thirty-two failed in English, and two hundred and thirty-four in arithmetic. From investigations entered into by authority at Dublin, it appears that the youths belonging to the middle classes in Ireland are so imperfectly educated, that it is with difficulty bankers and merchants can obtain an adequate supply of clerks. Their greatest deficiencies, as in the case of the Indian military students, are chiefly in English and arithmetic. The Dean of Hereford, however, from a personal inspection of the Irish schools for the humbler classes, argues very favourably of the prospects of education in Ireland. The plan of teaching there adopted is in fact so good, that it may serve as a model for the humbler schools of this country.

On the subject of schools for grown-up persons, there exists a variety of opinions. The Duke of Newcastle, in his famous Retford speech, told the good folks who listened to him that they were beginning at the wrong end, and that, instead of attacking the brains of adults, they ought to establish schools for children. But he should have remem-

bered the old proverb, "Better late than never."
Children, of course, should be educated, because,
when they are not, nothing can make up to them
for the want of what they ought to have acquired in
childhood. Yet it would be unreasonable to neglect
a man's youth because his childhood had been
neglected.

At one of the meetings of the Hants and Wilts
Society, held in the autumn of 1856, at Basingstoke, much light was thrown on the working of
the plan first put in operation by Dr. Dawes.
Among the suggestions made on that occasion by
the same excellent man, there was one which de-
served and has met with great attention. Having
noticed in the manufacturing districts, which have
always been foremost in civilization, the practice of
setting children to work during half the day, and
giving up the remainder to study, he suggested that
a modification of this half-time system might be
introduced into the agricultural districts. Instead
of dividing the day between labour and study, it
would then be necessary to appropriate alternate days
to those things; and although some difficulty may
be experienced in the attempt to realize this scheme,
that difficulty will certainly have to be overcome.

Everybody, of course, knows that the labours of

the field are interrupted by bad weather, and by the shortness of the days in winter. During these natural breaks in the operations of agriculture, the school-master might seize upon the children, and give them a taste of his quality. But in order thoroughly to diffuse knowledge among the peasantry, agricultural schools must be established in every part of the country.

The people of Great Britain have always been remarkable for their rural tastes, for their attachment to the fields, to the woods, to green lanes, to the wild sea-beach. Let them continue to be so, and let education foster the feelings which nature has implanted. In our literature and in our art there is visible a much stronger attachment to external nature than in those of any other country except Greece. Our poets seldom touch us more surely than when they speak of the woods and fields, when their verses abound with rural imagery, when the rippling of streams, the songs of birds, and the melancholy sighing of winds breathe through their verses.

Shakespeare, beyond all others, is an example of this truth. His works, in fact, may be regarded as an infinite series of landscapes, glimpses of woodland scenery, dewy glades, fairy rings, and moonlit val-leys. This, almost as much as anything, endears him to the English people. There is scarcely any object peculiarly beautiful in nature which he has not contrived to associate with his grand exhibitions of human passion. Accordingly, while we admire other writers, we love Shakespeare, who may almost be said to have educated the English nation, as Homer educated the Greeks.

To some extent, though in an infinitely smaller degree, our artists have worked upon the same principle, that is, have addicted themselves chiefly to landscape. Whoever loves the grand and terrible must seek in other lands, in deserts, in vast ranges of mountains, in wild and savage forests, food for his imagination ; but the lover of what I may almost call domestic beauty, scenes of unobtrusive loveliness, springs, groves, haunted streams, glades sprinkled with wild flowers, and moist with dew, lakes of unambitious softness, hills wreathed with mist, expanses of country dotted with frequent hamlets and church-spires, which impart a sort of religious aspect to nature,—the lover of these things, I say, will find in England more to delight and satisfy his mind than in any other country, Italy perhaps excepted.

To study agriculture is to study how to make the most of this beautiful country. No doubt the present race of farmers are well enough acquainted with their own business, as far as it has already been improved; but the great use of agricultural schools would be to suggest fresh improvements, to discover by experiment whether any new animals, trees, fruits, plants, birds, or fishes might be introduced, and what would be the extent of the advantages arising from their introduction.

There is a prejudice among us, which has been for some time steadily growing, against the languages of old Greece and Rome, with which it is certainly not necessary that farmers should be acquainted; but the discovery of the most powerful and valuable modern manures might have been made many centuries earlier, had men of a practical and suggestive character been in the habit of reading Hellenic authors for the purpose of deriving instruction from them.

The stimulating and fertilizing properties of guano were well known to the farmers of Hellas; and perhaps it would still be possible, by diligently studying the methods they pursued in the culture of the soil, to light upon other useful hints.

It was mentioned by a speaker at the Basingstoke meeting, among agricultural desiderata, that we want a reaping-machine. It would, perhaps, be too much to expect to find in ancient writers the description of one exactly suited to our purpose; but, by carefully considering the following passage, we may, perhaps, be led to the discovery of what we are in search of.

" In some parts of ancient Gaul, where no value was set upon the straw, corn was reaped by a sort of cart armed in front with scythes, having the edges inclined upwards, which, as it was driven along by an ox harnessed behind, cut off the ears of corn, which were received into the tumbril. In this manner the produce of a whole field might be got in easily in a day."*

If we substitute a steam-engine for the ox, and make it run on broad rollers instead of wheels, that it may not sink into the earth, we have before us the model of a complete reaping-machine. By sloping passages on both sides of the engine, the corn might be made to fall out behind, ready to be bound into sheaves.

But, of course, the most profitable studies for an agricultural population, are those which belong to the present state of things, the sciences connected with their profession, such as botany, chemistry, meteorology and natural history. It is obvious that they ought to be acquainted with the dispositions, powers, and peculiarities of all the animals which assist them in their labours,—the horse, the ox, the

* Ancient Greece, ii. 392. Palladius, 146.

dog. They ought also to be familiar with the nature
of all the animals they rear, as well as with that of
all English birds and insects. I do not doubt that
science will enable man to destroy all such insects
as are hurtful to him. Perhaps the substances are
lying plentifully around us, which, properly applied,
would exterminate the fly, and preserve all cereals,
roots, and vegetables from disease and blight. In
large agricultural institutions, all these things might
be taught, to some slightly, to others a little more
completely, and to a few thoroughly.

Few branches of study appear better calculated to
find favour with the humbler classes than botany.
Dr. Dawes, whom I have so often quoted, observes
" that a knowledge of the wild flowers of a district
may be turned to good account. In a visit which I
made to Manchester not long ago, I was astonished
to find among the operatives the knowledge of botany which many of them have, and the interest which
they take in this department of Natural History.
What healthful occupation this affords for a leisure
hour in various seasons of the year, in seeking for
particular plants, and seeing them in their own native
places !"

Our neighbours the French, though an agricultural people, are not much given to rural studies.

They work in the fields because it is their calling; but their general poverty and ignorance disincline them to prosecute even such investigations as seem most closely connected with their habitual pursuits.

I never met a French peasant who could tell me anything about the trees, plants, or flowers of his district. The ready reply to all questions was, " You see, Sir, it is not my business."

The Swiss, though not much better instructed, display a superior degree of curiosity. They dwell with a sort of unintelligible pleasure on the wild plants and flowers of the Alps. I have often seen, in early spring, a peasant watching on the verge of the snow for the first tiny wild flowers that appeared among the young grass, and exhibiting tokens of extreme delight when he discovered any. Again, in autumn, among the passes of the higher mountains, the same class of persons show much familiarity with the wild berries peculiar to those regions.

I remember once, when going to Italy in September, observing a valley in the Upper Alps looking as if it were almost on fire, with the flame-coloured leaves of a plant which the Swiss call Embrok. It produces a very sweet berry, in shape like the whortle, but of more delicate taste. Poverty is everywhere a great foe to the acquisition of knowledge;

but in the East I have known very poor persons who
were fond of flowers, and would dwell on their beauty
with more rapture, perhaps, than Linnæus himself
ever experienced. This, of course, was not science,
to which, however, under favourable circumstances
it might have led.

On the necks and arms of several Arab women I
have seen admirable representations, in tattoo-work, of
Egyptian flowers, among which was the Nilotic lotus.

Throughout the valley the peasants seem peculiarly addicted to botany, especially in Nubia, where
they study, with much care, the medicinal properties of plants. They have found out also, by experiment, what roots and berries are good for food,
and pointed out to me one large shrub which bears
an excellent substitute for coffee. They had a notion,
also, that the exquisitely lustrous and downy sub-
stance which fills, when ripe, the apple of the silk-
tree, might be turned to account in manufactures ;
and if it could, I think fabrics might be woven from
it more beautiful than the finest silks or shawls of
Cashmere.

I threw out this suggestion many years ago, though
it has not yet, I believe, been acted upon. If the silk
of the Asheyr should be found by experiment capable
of being worked up into garments, the discovery

would probably cause a complete revolution in the social condition of Egypt and Nubia, where it might be cultivated to almost any extent over a space of eight or nine hundred miles. It is found also in the Lower Valley of Jordan, where, however, the soil is less adapted to bring it to perfection than on the banks of the Nile. I have tried to rear the Asheyr from seeds in England; but on the first approach of autumn the plants completely melted and disappeared, as if they had been formed of dew.

There appears to be no reason why all the children of our rural districts should not be brought up in an agricultural school, since the humblest labourers would be rendered wiser, better, and more skilful, happier in themselves, and more valuable to their employers.

The great objection, no doubt, is the early age at which the children of the poor must be withdrawn from all kinds of schools, to be employed in productive labour. Burke, when he first came to England, went down to the manufacturing towns of Wiltshire, and was agreeably surprised that children even of the tenderest age were in those places rendered useful, as he expresses it, to their parents. It did not occur to his mind, that they would be thus rendered less useful afterwards to themselves.

The Duke of Newcastle, in a speech delivered at Newark, at the founding of the Christ Church Schools, mentioned a fact which may be regarded as a proof that education is at a low ebb in Nottinghamshire. In 1856 there were, it appears, no more than four-teen certificated teachers in the whole county, while the schools that existed were not more than half filled. The cause his Grace assigns is a strange one, namely, the great prosperity of the country, which creates an immense demand for infant labour. But if the country be prosperous, the prosperity must extend to the parents of the infants, and render it unnecessary for them to sacrifice their children.   In this case they are not actuated by poverty, but avarice.   But I dis-trust his Grace's facts.   The upper classes are pros-perous; but though the poor find employment, it is not sufficiently remunerative to render them independent of their children's aid.   The parents must be enabled to do without their children's wages, that is, must get more themselves.   If his Grace, or any one else, can show how this is to be done, he will indeed be a bene-factor to his country; but until the discovery is made, it is greatly to be feared that the schoolmaster will walk abroad in vain; the educational dispensaries, like those of Nottinghamshire, will remain half empty. The great necessity of the time is to invent some means of improving permanently the condition of the working classes; and this, it appears to me, is to be in a great measure effected by facilitating the acquisition of small portions of land by the poor.

But, however much we may lament it, the children of poor parents must early be taken away from study, because their time may be turned into money, which is wanted in their father's house. Still, in many, the slightest instruction given in childhood will fix for ever in the mind the love of study, and lead to the pursuit of it, during leisure hours, for the whole remainder of life. I do not agree with Lord Stanley in thinking that four hours a week are as good as forty, for strengthening and furnishing the mind; but if people could be induced to give up to learning the hours they now waste in idleness or in worse, a great deal might be done towards civilizing the working classes.

To render this more practicable and easy, the agricultural schools should always be open till a late hour in the evening. We are not to suppose that the cultivators of the soil need to be taught nothing but what is connected with their business. They have souls like other people, and therefore should be encouraged to acquaint themselves with the truths of religion; they are fathers, husbands, children, and need to be familiarized with the laws of morality; they are free men and citizens, and consequently ought to be acquainted with history and politics; they are men, and therefore need to know as much as possible of whatever interests mankind.

It is impossible not to agree with the Dean of Hereford in thinking that great advantage will be derived from educating the children of the farmers, the labourers, and the smaller tradesman at the same school. The moral and social advantages to be derived from this practice it would be difficult to exaggerate. It prevails already in Switzerland and several parts of Germany, and with the best possible results. From the same school emerge employers and employed, buyers and sellers. They know each other, have perhaps formed habits of friendship, or acquired sentiments of mutual esteem; and persons so circumstanced are most likely in after-life to become good neighbours, kind and considerate towards each other, and as far disinterested as the necessities of life will allow.

CHAPTER XV.

SCHOOLS OF EMIGRATION.

Density of Population.—The Strong kill the Weak, or force them
to emigrate.—Peopling of the Wilderness, carried on without
System.—Timidity of Ignorance ; how to be removed.—Wealth of
our Distant Provinces.—Pastoral Life.—Agriculture.—Mining.—
Common Trades.—Colonization of India.—Varieties of Soil and
Climate.—Long Life of English in India.—Ferocity of Mercenary
Troops.—New Zealand.—Dread of the Unknown.—Possible Population of Great Britain.—People too Numerous at present.—Increase of Crime.—Right of the State.—What restrains Emigration.
—Industrial Schools.—Sir John Pakington.—Anecdote of a Home-
less Boy.—Motives to Emigration.—Foundlings.—Excess of Female
Population.—How to be disposed of.—Men Invade the Employ-
ments of Women.—Economical Arguments for Emigration.

THERE is a natural tendency in mankind, when population overpasses certain limits, to abandon their
country and seek a new home elsewhere. The motive
to this expatriation is not always the impossibility of
finding food and employment, but the sense of too
great proximity, diffused through the whole people.
Trees, in a forest, become slender and weak when they
grow too close together ; and when some of a more

hardy nature develope themselves into their due pro-
portions, they stunt and wither, or kill altogether,
the smaller and weaker trees in their neighbourhood.

It is much the same in civil society. When certain
individuals of active and vigorous character absorb
more wealth and influence than should perhaps belong
to them, other persons are deprived of their due share,
and must either dwindle away and perish, or remove
to a distance from their more robust competitors.
This in all countries leads to conquest or emigration.
If there be space in the surrounding regions, the citizens of the thickly-peopled state cultivate martial
habits, and surge out upon their neighbours; if not,
they take to the sea and emigrate to new lands.

The latter is our case; after filling these islands
with an active and enterprising population, we have
gone to the remotest parts of the earth in search of
new settlements.

But this process has not been conducted upon
just and wise principles. From the founding of our
first colony to the present day, we have obeyed our
instincts rather than our reason, and poured forth
swarms of emigrants, good and bad, suited and unsuited, to people the wildernesses of America, Africa,
and Australasia.

Success however, it may be said, has crowned our

efforts. True ; but the success would have been much greater, and the suffering and misery by which it has been purchased infinitely less, had we acted from the beginning upon a rational system of emigration.

It is not too late to have recourse to such a system now ; and the first step towards organizing it would be to establish Schools of Emigration. The object of such establishments would be to diffuse through the country correct ideas of our possessions. Thousands, who have not bread to eat in this country, cling to it desperately nevertheless, because their minds are filled with indefinite fears whenever Canada or the Cape or New Zealand is mentioned. They could not, if questioned, give any satisfactory reason for the apprehensions they feel. Their energies however are, obviously, paralyzed by nothing but ignorance. If they knew more about our colonies, they would only be too happy to exchange indigence at home for plenty, perhaps opulence, in one of our dependencies.

To remove this unwillingness to inhabit the remoter parts of the empire, it is necessary to diffuse instruction respecting those provinces through all classes of the community, and more especially among the poor. In the first place, they should be taught to regard a ship merely as a floating bridge connecting the various parts of the empire. Over this bridge they may step to any British province they please. If they dislike their new settlement, the same bridge always exists to take them to another, or back to the old country.

As nobody can deny that it is desirable to people those rich countries which Providence has given to us in different parts of the world, it is clear that we ought to inform ourselves about all the circumstances by which each of them is characterized.

In this case it is not mere geographical knowledge that will suffice. The information which the student is in search of is of a more homely kind. He wants to discover where he can best find a field suited at once to his taste and his means. In some colonies a man may most profitably betake himself to the pastoral life, in others to agriculture, in others to mining, and in others, again, to the ordinary trades and callings prevalent in the mother-country.

At a school of emigration, children, youths, and adults might be familiarized with all these facts; they would learn the natural history of every colony, and be taught to estimate its capabilities and suitableness or unsuitableness to their own capacity.

When persons possess extensive knowledge respecting any place, provided it be tolerably healthy, they have seldom any reluctance to go to it. Suppose, for example, it were determined to colonize India, it would be necessary in the first place to get rid of the idea that it is totally unsuited to the constitution of Englishmen. Being a very large country, and lying consequently under many parallels of latitude, its climate must necessarily be different in different parts. Besides, in some divisions there are lofty mountains clothed with primeval forests; in others, hills and valleys, beautifully diversified; in others, rich plains or sandy deserts. In a region so vast, and of so varied an aspect and character, it is perfectly obvious that persons of all kinds of temperaments may settle with safety.

But, to create this belief, it is necessary to diffuse a certain amount of instruction. Examples may be mentioned of English people who have attained to a great old-age in India, brought up large families, and bequeathed a sound and vigorous constitution to their children. What has happened in many instances, people will infer is likely to happen again ; and their chief objection to settling in that part of the empire will be removed.

There exists, however, in the minds of many persons another strong objection,—I mean the difference of language ; but this need not long retain any force if the British Government think proper to do away

with it. The Hindús display a remarkable aptitude
for the acquisition of English, which, when they have
been carefully taught, they speak without the slightest
Asiatic accent, and so correctly that, if you heard an
English and a Hindú gentleman converse together
in the dark, you would not be able to tell which was
which.

In this respect they are far superior to the Scotch
and Irish, and even to the natives of many English
counties, who seldom or never lose altogether their
provincial accent. This remark appears not to be
applicable to the Mohammedans, whose vocal organs
are so much less flexible, that a Hindú child of five
years old will often surpass a Musulman of five-and-
twenty in the knowledge and pronunciation of our
language.

But, among persons of all classes, the taste for acquiring the language of the ruling caste is spreading
rapidly through India, where it is said that not less
than thirty thousand persons, and perhaps a great
many more, are actively engaged in mastering the
difficulties of our mother-tongue. The pupils of the
missionaries in the various provinces have been calculated to exceed a hundred thousand ; but these, though
taught the rudiments of Western civilization, are not
anywhere, I believe, instructed in our language.   To

this number we may add twenty-five or thirty thousand who are educated in the Government schools.

In 1844 Lord Hardinge established a hundred village schools for instruction in the native languages; but though the motive which led to their foundation was praiseworthy, the scheme itself must have been somehow very defective, since about half the number were soon closed, and very little good was effected by the remainder. Government has since modified, though it has not altogether abandoned, Lord Hardinge's system; its plan still embraces education in the vernacular for the mass of the people, and English education for the upper classes, that is, for such of the natives of great towns as desire and can afford to pay for it.

However, the sort of education given in what are called the vernacular schools, is of a very low character, and therefore not at all calculated to improve or enlarge the national mind. The native works employed, when not in every way abominable, are still worthless. Several of our countrymen, in order to supply a better class of books, have made translations of some of our own authors into the vernacular; but these are pronounced, by a very competent authority, to be ludicrously bad. One learned Pundit undertook to translate Addison into Bengalee; and it would

be difficult to imagine more grotesque figures than
Sir Roger de Coverley and Will Honeycomb in their
Bengalee dress.   But the intrepidity of translators
on the banks of the Ganges, whether indigenous or
imported, is prodigious; and nobody can doubt that,
with adequate pecuniary encouragement, a host of
gentlemen, both English and Hindú, would step forward at once and undertake to translate Shakespeare
for the benefit of young Brahmans, both male and
female.

It is admitted throughout Asia that the natives of
India, and more especially of Bengal, are distinguished for superior intelligence; but their religion,
and the manners to which it gives birth, interfere
greatly with the development of the intellect, and
cause men who were brilliant students in youth, not
only to fall short in after-life of the promise of their
spring, but to become as remarkable for the inertness
of their minds as they had once been for logical or
imaginative power.

While the English, however, continue masters of
India, the work of instruction will undoubtedly go on.
Our Asiatic empire itself arose out of small beginnings; and therefore we may hope that, on a foundation equally slender, knowledge will hereafter erect
for itself an empire in the same land. I do not under-

take to mention here all that has been done for education by the English in India, but merely to notice a few prominent points. Among the existing establishments are :—

The Metropolitan College; Principal, Mr. D. L.

Richardson; * number of students   . . .   600
The Residency College 132
School depending on it 462
The Government College 339
The Calcutta Medressy 170
Madras School or University, supported by Government.

Both in this latter Presidency, and throughout the rest of India and Ceylon, there are numerous missionary schools. The teachers themselves amount to about 400, to whom must be added 1,600 native agents. Of these, only about thirty are clergymen. The number of missionary societies is about twenty-two, and by these the Bible has been translated into ten of the principal languages of India.

Our recent experience of the ferocity of certain

* Mr. Richardson's experience and long residence in India qualify him to supply very valuable information respecting the state of education in that country. He is familiarly acquainted both with Hindús and Mohammedans, having been engaged for years in the task of enlightening their minds; and therefore, if he were to write a book on the mental condition of the natives of our Asiatic empire, I think it would be well received in this country.

classes among the natives need not alarm us for the future. The history of Europe proves that mercenary troops, ready, for pay, to do the bidding of any master, are generally gifted with very little humanity, and have in all ages and countries perpetrated crimes akin to those which the Muslim and Hindú sipahis have committed against us.

Not many years ago, people had the strongest possible objection to settle in New Zealand, chiefly because the natives were cannibals. Sydney Smith's joke about breakfasting on cold missionary made the circuit of our islands, and diffused immense horror; but when experience at length showed that both missionaries and settlers not only escaped being eaten, but in general got much better things to eat than they could have obtained in their own country, the prejudice against that beautiful colony rapidly wore away. The unknown is always dreaded. Perhaps death itself appears terrible only because we cannot beforehand assure ourselves to what it leads. A thorough acquaintance with the regions beyond the grave might make mankind so desirous of reaching them, that they would adopt all possible methods of leaving the world, which may be the reason why impenetrable darkness is suffered to hang over the future.

Some ingenious writers have maintained that the British Islands, under the influence of different institutions, might sustain a population four times as great as the present. This may or may not be true, and it is of little consequence to us whether it be so or not, because with the institutions we have it is quite clear such a state of things is impossible. We find, by daily experience, that there exists around and in the midst of us a surplus population, which, on account of the difficulty of getting an honest livelihood, betakes itself to every form of dishonesty. To this surplus seven or eight thousand children are added every year, from which we may reasonably infer that in the course of time the whole mass of the working people will be tainted.

I am not by any means favourable to the invasion of personal liberty, but I maintain that the State has a right to locate upon any part of its dominions it pleases those who have in any way infringed its laws. Properly speaking, however, this consideration does not connect itself with my present subject. I only desire to prove that there exist in these islands large numbers of persons who would gladly emigrate if they only knew the nature and condition of our several colonies. Acts of Parliament have been passed both for England and Scotland, rendering it lawful for magistrates to commit to school, instead of prison, children found guilty of acts of vagrancy in the public streets.

Sir John Pakington tells an anecdote of a boy he once met in the streets of Worcester begging. He inquired of the lad about his home and his parents, and was told that he had none. " Where and how do you live, then?" inquired Sir John. "Where I can," replied the boy; " and I begs as long as people will give me anything, and when they won't I steals."

This boy represents a large class, upon which the industrial schools are intended to operate. They are to be taught various trades and callings, and then let loose to compete in a labour-market which is already overstocked with competitors. Let those industrial schools be converted into schools of emigration, and let the children of both sexes who are brought up in them be educated exclusively with a view to the Colonies. Again, a great number of our poor who are shut up in workhouses, when strong and youthful, would emigrate if proper means were taken to induce them. It would also be a wise and humane thing to receive at emigration-schools all foundlings, and educate them for the colonies. This, in a great measure, would preserve the nation from the crime of infanticide, by transferring that life, which is a drug here, to places where it would be of immense value both to itself and others.

To facilitate this, and prevent their desertion and death, there should be attached to all these schools an establishment for the reception of infants, to whomsoever they might belong. As in other countries, they might be introduced through a turning box, with the utmost secrecy, at night, a bell being touched to give notice of the approach of an inmate. Once in, the child should belong to the Colonies, and be educated accordingly. Indeed the only way to render Foundling Hospitals useful is to convert them into seminaries of emigration; and I feel convinced that, if this were done, the Colonies would in a short time consent to bear all the expense, in consideration of the valuable additions which might thus be made to their industrial population. The boys should be brought up to trades, and the girls properly instructed for performing the duties of domestic servants. At the age of fourteen, both might be forwarded to their place of destination, and become a blessing to their new country and to themselves. This plan, I repeat, if properly realized, would put an end to infanticide, and remove from our civilization one of its worst stains, since no one could have the slightest temptation to de-

stroy a child, of which the State would willingly
become the fostering parent. To ensure diligence
and kindness in the managers, their salaries should
be regulated by the proportion of children reared
in health to the age of fourteen, and fitted by instruction and training to perform the duties of their
station.

One of the most difficult questions connected with
this subject is how women are to be expatriated in
sufficient numbers.   From the last census, it appears
that the excess of females over males in the British
Islands does not fall greatly short of one million.   In
several of our colonies, on the other hand, the excess
of males over females is said to be almost as four to
one.   To remedy this state of things, it is clearly necessary that there should be more female than male
emigrants. But women generally are less enterprising
than men, and are, above all things, reluctant to go
forth into the wide world without a protector.   If
they were brought up' at emigration-schools, and had
their minds habituated from childhood to look upon
some colony as their home, they would experience
very little unwillingness, when grown up, to proceed
to that home.

Here, they would perceive, it is difficult to obtain
respectable employment, and, for tens of thousands,

altogether impossible to reckon on marriage. Owing to the perverse tastes of society, men in numerous instances betake themselves to female employments, and thus deteriorate the condition of those who were but too wretched before.

The chief objection in all cases of this kind is the expense; but already the State is compelled to provide for the education and maintenance of large numbers of children in industrial schools, in national schools, and in reformatories. The cost of police magistrates and prisons would be immensely reduced if the population were brought down to its proper level. Ignorance and idleness are the parents of policemen, magistrates, and gaolers. What you expend on emigration you save, therefore, in these items, while it is perfectly certain that the multiplication of colonists augments the demand for our manufactures, and thus enriches that portion of the population which remains at home.

That it would be easy to raise objections against everything I have said, it is impossible to doubt. No scheme was ever proposed for the adoption of mankind, which ingenious persons would not undertake to prove to be impracticable: but there are few things that may not by energy and perseverance be accomplished; and the act of delivering Great

Britain from its surplus population would, in my opinion, be found easy, if undertaken in a proper spirit by the Government, and approved by public opinion.

CHAPTER XVI.

STUDIES OF EMIGRANTS.

Studies of Emigrants.—Influence of Names.— Inducements to settle
in New Brunswick.—Millions of Acres for Sale.—Great Cheapness
of Land.— Hills, Valleys, and Forests.—Health of the Inhabit-
ants.—Forest Trees.—Fisheries.—Abundance of Game.—Proli-
ficness of the Ocean ; how to be turned to account.—Location of
Emigration Schools.—Modes of Instruction.—Maps.—Views.—
Objects of Natural History.—Physical Geography. —History of
Early Settlers.—The Promised Land.—Delusions of Ignorance.—
The Englishman finds England everywhere.—His beloved Box.—
Growth of New Towns.—The Wilderness sanctified by Religion.

CIRCUMSTANCES have lately tended to render widely
known the colonies of Australia and New Zealand.
Canada also, and the Cape of Good Hope, have
attracted a considerable share of attention. But
there is a very pleasant and interesting colony in a
corner of North America, which deserves much more
notice than has been bestowed upon it.

Whatever may be said to the contrary, we are so
imaginative a people, that suggestive, musical, and
strange names exercise great influence over us even
when we are looking out for a comfortable home in

some distant part of the British dominions. Among the provinces of the United States there are some whose very names have a powerful fascination—Illinois, Alabama, Missouri, Pennsylvania, Virginia, Delaware, Maryland.

But New Brunswick has nothing whatever to recommend it as an appellation. Even for Old Brunswick nobody cares, except those Germans who inhabit it; consequently it would be too much to expect that a district in the New World, lying moreover a good deal out of the great highway of commerce, would become very attractive from being named after a highly uninteresting part of the Continent. Still in itself New Brunswick holds out many inducements for Englishmen to settle in it.*

From the latest accounts we find that there are seven millions five hundred thousand acres of good land in the colony still unsold. On these, therefore, an immense number of persons, in want of some place to call their own, might settle and make themselves comfortable. The utmost extent of territory they can ever reckon upon possessing in this country is six feet by two, and even this they can hardly count upon possessing in peace; but in the snug little colony of which I am speaking, they might purchase a whole

* See Mr. Perley's excellent little Handbook on New Brunswick.

acre for two shillings and threepence, or even get it
without money for a certain quantity of labour.

New Brunswick, like a surly but good-natured
man, frowns upon the new comers. Its Atlantic
shores are rocky and forbidding; but if you are not
daunted by this circumstance, and make up your
mind to go inland, you meet with innumerable beautiful valleys, rivers, and hills, with an extent of virgin
forest calculated to delight your fancy. You are very
far, however, from finding yourself in a wilderness,
but observe on all sides towns, villages, and hamlets,
with good roads and capital bridges, churches, colleges, schools, and all the apparatus of civilization.

The health and ruddy complexions of the inhabitants reveal the salubrity of the climate, which will
be still further increased by the operations of the axe
and the plough. In the forests of this province are
found trees of the most majestic and useful character,
—the white pine, the black spruce, the American
larch, the birch, the beech, and the maple. The lakes,
streams, and bays abound with fish of various kinds,
and thousands earn a handsome livelihood by catch-
ing and curing them.

At an earlier period of our history, if such a country
had been laid open to enterprise, and the proper degree of information respecting it diffused, the swarms

of settlers would, in all likelihood, have been much greater. A man of hardy habits might almost live entirely by his fowling-piece, since game of all kinds abounds in every forest,—moose, reindeer, the Virginian red deer, the beaver, the otter, the sable, and the ermine. Wild ducks and wild geese, the passenger pigeon, snipe, and woodcock, are found in great plenty.

The inhabitants of the earth might almost subsist upon the inhabitants of the ocean, if the proper amount of industry were devoted to the innumerable fisheries of the world. The youth, therefore, proceeding to colonies on the shores of which fish abound, should be accustomed from childhood to the sea. They should be taught the management of boats, the making of sails, of twine, of nets, of harpoons and all other instruments used in striking large fish. Already the wealth of the Gulf of St. Lawrence, the Bay of Fundy, the banks of Newfoundland, and many other bays, gulfs, and creeks are known to the world; but, much as we are given to navigation and all its auxiliary practices and callings, we are very far from having explored all the sources of opulence to be found in the sea. What is already known, however, would suffice, if actively turned to account, to employ many thousands of hands now withering in idleness, or held out in the streets to grasp the pittance doled forth by charity, or stretched, thin and meagre, over the workhouse table, to reach the scanty and thoroughly-grudged food supplied by the parish.

If the schools I recommend should ever be established, some of them should be built in mining, some in rural districts, some on the sea-coast; and they should be always kept open in the evening, that the young people of the neighbourhood might be able to frequent them. A part of the instruction might be conveyed orally, in familiar conversation rather than in lectures. Adults, whose curiosity had been awakened, would ask questions which, in many cases, might be answered by the more advanced pupils, or by the schoolmasters and schoolmistresses. Use should also be made of lectures, with maps, views, engravings of animals, trees, and plants. Information should be given respecting the climate, the degrees of heat and cold, the prevalent winds, the march of the seasons, and the effect of all these combined influences on human life. It would be well also to familiarize the frequenters of these schools with the history of the first settlers in America : how they went away back into the woods; how they felled the trees; how they built themselves log huts ; and how they cleared the first plot of ground for the reception of wheat or barley.

The schools in which this kind of knowledge should be taught would soon come to possess extraordinary interest for the poor, as they would open up before their minds a prospect of the promised land, where every one by industry might become the proprietor of fields or vineyards, vast tracks of pasturage for sheep, woods for timber, or meadows for cattle.

Persons wholly unfamiliar with those parts of the empire are apt to represent them to themselves as mighty and trackless wildernesses, where the unhappy emigrants who venture into them must be deprived of all social intercourse, and even of the blessings of religion. A short attendance at an emigration-school would destroy these delusions : they would learn to measure the distance between the central provinces and those lying upon the skirts of our dominions, not by thousands of miles, but by weeks or days. They would next make the discovery, that the Englishman carries England along with him wherever he goes.

No sooner has he made a clearance in the wilderness, than he sets himself about reproducing the ugly but beloved architecture of his native land. A box set on end, pierced here and there with square holes to let in the light, is his house, and a large number of these boxes constitutes a town. Here he has his police station, his courts of law and justice, his schools, his academies, and, above all, his churches; these, with their towering spires reddened by the rising or setting sun, impart sacredness and beauty to the landscape. The bells ring on Sunday morning, and multitudes of people stream, as in the old country, towards the building, which begins to look venerable the moment it is finished. There the same prayers are offered up, the same hymns sung, the same sermons preached. Trees of new growth and strange foliage cluster about the building which people soon learn to look upon as the vestibule of heaven. Under that roof they no longer regret their old homes in the north, and learn to feel the grand truth that God is present everywhere, and that wherever He is, is the home of man's soul.

CHAPTER XVII.

MECHANICS' INSTITUTES.

IT is a pretty general opinion that the experiment of enlightening the working classes, by means of Mechanics' Institutes, has entirely failed. The number of these establishments, it is admitted, is very considerable, and the attendance, upon the whole, good. But this, it is said, proves nothing, because the members in most cases are not mechanics or belonging to the humbler classes at all. Lord Brougham, one of their

originators, admitted, not long ago, in a speech at
Birmingham, that he had been entirely disappointed
in his hopes, and mentioned, by way of illustration,
one Institute which, with six hundred members, had
only twenty-four mechanics among them.

This account certainly appears discouraging. The
censure, however, does not rest altogether with the mechanics. The principles upon which those institutions
were at first based contained a fundamental error,
which, in spite of the ability and excellent intentions
of their founders, has so greatly circumscribed the
good they were designed to produce, as almost entirely
to frustrate the expectations of the country. Lord
Brougham, Dr. Birkbeck, and many others wish to
inoculate the great body of the people with an absorbing passion for science.* I don't know that even
the wish was wise; but at any rate it was easy to
foresee from the beginning that it would prove fruit-
less. No large class of men was ever actuated by
such a feeling; and therefore to suppose that they who
spend the greater part of their lives in labour might

* The Duke of Newcastle, in his speech to the operatives of Retford,
reckons, among the causes of the failure of Mechanics' Institutes,
the attempt to introduce into them too much of the arts and sciences.
This judicious observation is followed by another, which may provoke
a smile : his Grace allows that Shakespeare and works of a similar
kind may be read. Shakespeare is the greatest master of human
wisdom known to the modern world ; and therefore, instead of saying

be imbued with it, was to lose sight altogether of the conditions of human nature.

The people want many things besides science. Above all they want amusement, conversation, harmless excitement, and something to do during their leisure hours. It is unreasonable to expect that persons accustomed to manual exertions will, day after day, pass at one bound from carpentering, bricklaying, weaving, spinning, fabricating steam-engines, or forging anchors, to the solution of geometrical problems, or the abstruse investigations of astronomy. Grant even that the Mechanics' Institutes possess large libraries filled with entertaining books; these will not prove at all times a sufficient attraction for all classes of workmen. There are moments when people do not feel inclined to read, still less to study and be amused with diagrams.

What then is to be done? Change the character of the Institutes. They have been called the Poor Man's University; let them be also his clubhouse, his

---

that his works *may* be read, his Grace should have pointed out the immense advantages to be derived from the assiduous study of them. In the Working Men's and Working Women's Colleges founded by Professor Maurice, the readers of Shakespeare constitute a large class, which in all likelihood will every day become more numerous. I am surprised, however, that it should not have been thought desirable to associate with him the man who, as Coleridge expresses it, occupies the other glory-smitten summit of Parnassus.

theatre, the general scene of his recreations. Let there be coffee and smoking-rooms attached to every one of these establishments, and workmen will soon be found to frequent them in much greater numbers than at present. To improve the tastes and habits of the masses, it is not by any means necessary to appeal exclusively to the intellect. The physical part of man's nature requires to be attended to quite as much as the mental; and if it were not absolutely necessary, it would still be found useful to bring wisely and moderately into play the habits and predilections of the humbler classes. Precautions might easily be taken to prevent excess, though the influence of the public opinion which could not fail to exist would of itself be generally sufficient to ensure orderly and manly behaviour.

Another means of interesting the mechanics in their Institutes would be to include in them a shooting-gallery, a place for sword-exercise, for pitching the quoit, throwing the jereed, and many other forms of healthful exercise. These amusements would alternate agreeably with reading and study; and if they absorbed the greater part of the mechanic's time, they would still produce a beneficial effect upon his mind and manners. Our forefathers of all ranks addicted themselves to these recreations. It is related of Henry V., the greatest and best of our princes since the Conquest, that he was fond, from his earliest youth, of all manly exercises—wrestling, leaping, running, the casting of iron bars and heavy stones. While thus engaged, whether in rain or sunshine, he went bare-headed, and was ever ready to try his strength with persons of nearly all classes.

Some statesmen, observing the increase of studious tendencies, have been apprehensive that they might lead to effeminacy, and have therefore regretted that the savage sports once popular in England should have gone out of use. It is certain that familiarity with pain, blows, and wounds renders men fit for war; but it is scarcely necessary that they should be accustomed to inflict torture on the inferior animals —cocks, dogs, bulls, bears—to render them courageous in the field of battle.

Hitherto it is certain there has been no decay of valour in the English people. Sir James Kaye Shuttleworth, in a speech delivered at Preston, alludes, in proof of this, to the exploits of the Lancashire men in the Crimea; we may now point with still greater confidence to the plains of Hindustan, where not only our countrymen but our countrywomen have displayed a self-possession, an intrepidity, and a heroism which neither the Spartans nor the Romans, nor even our Puritan ancestors, ever excelled.

A few weeks, or even days, before the mutiny broke

out, any stranger who should have passed through
the Upper Provinces and visited the stations of the
English, might have inferred, from their easy, quiet,
and somewhat luxurious manners, that they had degenerated from their victorious forefathers of Plassy.
But neither Plassy nor Assaye, nor Marathon, nor
Platæa, nor any other battle ever fought on the surface of this planet, displayed greater qualities of mind
or heart than the new achievements of the English in
India. Women shielding their husbands' breasts with
their own bodies, men shooting their own wives to
preserve them from dishonour, ladies in the bloom of
youth throwing themselves by hundreds into the
Ganges though the same motive,—these and a thousand other examples of greatness of mind may be regarded as the triumphs of English education.

We obviously only need to persevere in the course
we have hitherto pursued, to preserve our ascendency
in the world. No portion of human history is more
glorious than the records of England during the pre-
ceding year; and I scarcely think it too much to say
that nothing can ever happen in future times to dim
by comparison the lustre of these brave deeds.

Many of the recreations of our ancestors promoted
strength and hardihood without encouraging cruelty;
and some of their amusements might be revived and

connected with Mechanics' Institutes with great advantage both to the health and morals of those who frequent them.   Sir James Kaye Shuttleworth, an active friend of education, and one who has done much to diffuse its blessings, while alluding to the lament of Wyndham over the decay of sanguinary pastimes, almost appears to insinuate that no pastimes are necessary.   But if these are his views, I can by no means concur with him.   All great nations, and those more especially which have distinguished themselves for superior intellect, have been strongly addicted to athletic exercises, both as a preparation for war, and as conducements to health.   The theory prevailing in the wisest ages taught that the greatest of human blessings is a sound mind in a sound body; and they were thoroughly persuaded that, where the body is unsound, the mind can rarely be otherwise.

If these convictions had regulated the originators of Mechanics' Institutes, they would have met with much greater success than they have yet obtained. It is, I fear, but too true that the entire number of their members does not exceed one hundred thousand, whereas, had they been differently constituted, it would probably by this time have exceeded a million.   Whenever a war breaks out, the utter ignorance of the population, in everything relating to the use of arms, is made painfully evident. Mechanics in general know as little how to use a rifle or a sword as a quadrant or a telescope, whereas they should be as familiar with both as with the way to parish church. Historians have stated it as the reason for the unrivalled skill of the English archers,* that the whole male population of England was from the cradle accustomed to the use of the bow. For the bow we should now substitute the rifle, in the use of which every man in England should be skilful. While I lived in Switzerland I used frequently to go out on Sunday to see the young men practise with the rifle, and noticed that great numbers of them were remarkable for the trueness of their aim and their extreme fondness for the practice. All the women of the neighbourhood assembled to witness their achievements; and among them the successful marksman was a great favourite. It is this custom, in part at least, that renders the Swiss so independent, fearless, and formidable to the surrounding despotisms.

We are often reproached, as a nation, with too great a fondness for the practical, but without reason. There may be, and no doubt are, great faults in our

* On the great importance of archery in the estimation of our ancestors, see Mr. George Hansard's 'Book of Archery,' the work of a real scholar, displaying a thorough knowledge of the subject, and filled with rare and interesting anecdotes.

mode of developing our ideas; but we are the most imaginative people in Europe, the least tied down to routine, as is proved by the facility with which we adopt new inventions. Yet sometimes we are addicted to taking too much of a good thing. It would be difficult to overrate the advantages accruing to society from the steam-engine; and it is therefore but reasonable that we, who were its inventors, and have applied it most extensively, should seek to make ourselves generally acquainted with its mechanism. But it must not be thought to be the God of the English people. There are other things needful to be understood besides the steam-engine; and among these I think should be reckoned the sword, the rifle, the cannon, the mortar, and everything appertaining to the defence of nations. All the preliminaries of actual war might be converted into amusement and exercise; and it would greatly enlarge the minds of youth to be instructed in the art of pitching and striking camps, making pontoons and flying bridges, manœuvring artillery, fortifying towns—in one word, everything which belongs to a military nation.

The heir of the House of Derby, who seems inclined to carry into the management of public business the free spirit displayed by his master Arnold in literature and theology, has made himself a sort of

reputation in connection with popular teaching, by a
speech which he delivered in 1856, at Oldham. In
that speech he traces out a very wide field for the
mind of the mechanic to move in, recommending him
to apply the powers of his mind to investigating the
laws of organic and inorganic matter, penetrating the
secrets of astronomy, and solving the problems of
what we are, and what is the universe in which we
find ourselves. All these tasks, he thinks, may be
accomplished by working men in the few hours left
them by their daily labours.

Stunned by the vastness of this scheme, others
have endeavoured to disparage the advantages of the
working classes, and inferred them to be capable of
accomplishing little more than the reading of novels
and a few commonplace works of biography and history. While passing judgment on mechanics, however, we should not lose sight of the other orders
of society. Of the noble and the opulent, what is the
proportion of those who distinguish themselves for
genius, for knowledge, or for anything else? Is it so
high as one in a thousand? I think not. Considering all the difficulties with which the working classes
have to contend, we ought to be quite satisfied if we
discover among them one-tenth of the capacity for
study possessed by those who have no other employ-

ment in life.   Accordingly, among the immense multitude of mechanics and labourers of all classes, we
should only look for a few examples here and there of
superior industry, leading to remarkable results.

Dr. Dawes, the Dean of Hereford, mentioned at a
meeting in Hampshire the case of a young miner,
who by the age of twenty-two, though passing the
greater part of his life underground, had taught himself the physical geography of the British Islands,
together with arithmetic, grammar, the history of
England, and a little French and Latin.   Again, at
Huddersfield, Dr. Booth spoke of a young man of the
same name with himself, who had gained the prize
awarded by a Mechanics' Institute, who had made
progress not only in grammar, history, and geography,
but likewise in geometry, music, and French.   This
youth, living at a distance from the town, and having to
work all day for his bread, nevertheless walked twelve
miles every evening, in order to continue his studies.

These, it must be acknowledged, are examples of
Anglo-Saxon energy, and I may add of Anglo-Saxon
taste, feeling, and perception of the beautiful.   It
would not be difficult to adduce many other examples.
But it is not to be supposed that all young men are
gifted with this energy and indomitable love of study;
but whether in high or low, rich or poor, these alone

are the qualities that can lead to distinction and eminence.   Examine the records of what profession soever
you may, you will find that they who have attained
celebrity have been content

"To scorn delights, and live laborious days."

Buffon observed to Hérault de Sechelles, that when
he was a young man in Paris, devoured by the thirst
of fame, he used to rise at five o'clock in the morning,
winter and summer, to pursue his studies.   Sometimes in the evening, the love of pleasure proving too
strong for the love of knowledge, he would go out to
parties, and return home as late perhaps as two o'clock
in the morning; but the hour of rising was still rigidly
the same.   "I awoke and got up if I could," he said;
"and if I could not, my Swiss valet, a very powerful
fellow, had orders to wake me, and lift me out of bed,
by force if necessary."   Health and the buoyancy of
youth soon enabled him to shake off drowsiness and
apply himself to his studies.

Mademoiselle Clairon, the celebrated actress, when
educating herself for the stage, devoted a considerable portion of time to the study of anatomy.   Her
object was to discover the action and power of all
those muscles which serve by their depression or pro-
minence to express the emotions of the mind.   Having
made great progress in this study, she one evening, at

a large party, seated herself in an arm-chair, and, without speaking or gesture, contrived by the mere play of her countenance to electrify all present by the most varied exhibitions of emotions and passions. She joyed, she grieved, she exulted, she bewailed, she threatened, dared, conciliated, was angry, and exhibited all the allurements of love. The spectators forgot where they were, transported themselves by their imagination to the theatre, and experienced all the excitement which the acting of a great play would have caused. When the actress rose and dispelled the illusion, all present predicted the unrivalled eminence to which she afterwards attained.

These examples, taken from very different classes, will afford an illustration of how much may be accomplished by the force of will and singleness of purpose. But there never was a nation composed of such individuals. The pre-eminence of some proves the inferiority of others. But because a man is less than great, he need not be altogether destitute of knowledge; and this in all kinds and degrees is desirable and valuable. If the mathematical student cannot be Newton, he may yet learn to comprehend the logic of the Principia. In poetry, too, hundreds of thousands who could not write 'Hamlet' or the 'Paradise Lost,' may yet derive lifelong pleasure from those mighty creations of genius; and these considerations ought to be sufficient to encourage the poor and lonely student to persevere in his labours.

In calculating the effect of Mechanics' Institutes on the students who frequent them, we must take into account the architectural character of the buildings themselves, which often possess an air of imposing grandeur. To this Lord Palmerston alluded in a speech delivered in the Free Trade Hall to the mechanics of Manchester. They possessed, he said, an edifice such as might be erected by an emperor of the present day, or have been bequeathed to us by one of the great commercial States of the Middle Ages.

Our minds are influenced in various ways. Religion itself comes to us with greater power in antique and vast cathedrals than in ordinary rooms; and therefore it cannot be doubted that secular knowledge will act more strongly upon the mind when it is connected with magnificent associations—spacious buildings, stained windows, statues, pictures, brilliant lights, and elegant furniture. All these the mechanic may enjoy at his Institute; and if there be added to them the charms of a noble literature, I can hardly conceive the nature of that understanding which could remain unimpressed in the midst of so many appeals to all its faculties.

CHAPTER XVIII.

INFLUENCE OF THE UPPER ON THE LOWER CLASSES.

Influence of the Upper on the Lower Classes.—Limited Intercourse.
—Efforts made by Persons of Rank.—Lord Palmerston, Sir Robert
Peel.—Barrier between Classes.—Difference of Language.—Voca-
bulary of the Poor ; to be studied by the Rich.—Various dialects
of England ; the Basis of our Language.—Interchange of Ideas
advantageous to Rich and Poor.—Savages and Peasants.—Lord
Robert Cecil, his erroneous Conclusions.—Foreign Languages.—
Influence of Foreign Climates.—Lower Orders and Despotisms.—
Turks and Frenchmen.—Uncouth Peasantry of England.—Their
Shrewdness and Good Sense.—The Northumbrians.—The Arab
and the Clock.—Experience of the Clergy.—Distinct Spheres of
Thought.—Mutual Study of the Classes.—The Language of the
Pulpit.—The Priest and his Congregation.

THEY who contemplate from a high theoretical point
of view the enlightenment and elevation of the people, rightly enough consider a certain amount of intercourse between the upper and lower classes as one
of the most efficient means of effecting this purpose.
Hitherto however this intercourse has been found
practicable only under very limited conditions. Persons of rank and fortune, actuated by the desire to

do good to their countrymen, have made their appearance at Public Libraries, Lyceums, and Mechanics' Institutes, and delivered something between lectures and speeches to audiences composed chiefly of the humbler classes.   Lord Palmerston, for example, has addressed to the people of Manchester his opinions on the diffusion of knowledge; the Duke of Newcastle has twice undertaken the task of enlightening the people of Retford; Sir Robert Peel at once instructed and amused the men of Birmingham by a narrative of his adventures in Russia; and Lord Ravensworth, who appears to be fond of disputation, excited the people of Blaydon by a discourse on theological polemics.   Lord John Russell also, at different times and in various places, has endeavoured to diffuse among the working classes his enlarged ideas on the subject of education.

The moment we bestow any consideration on the question, we begin to discover the numerous difficulties attending the intercourse between rich and poor. When the classes come together, each finds itself ignorant of the sentiments and modes of thinking of the other. This is set down almost entirely to the absence of knowledge among the poor.   But there is another side to the question.   There is also a deficiency in the education of the rich, who should regard it as a duty to make their education embrace a knowledge of the idiosyncrasies of their poorer neighbours. If the latter spoke a different language, as they do in parts of Ireland, Scotland, and Wales, it would be incumbent on the upper orders to learn that language, that they might be able to communicate freely with those beneath them in the social system. In fact, the poor do everywhere speak a dialect different from the rich. Their vocabulary is not only more limited, but the words themselves are often different. They project their ideas into phrases which have no meaning at all to the upper classes, who find accordingly, when they come to converse with the poor, that they do not possess the requisite medium.

It appears, therefore, that it is not only necessary to instruct the poor, that they may understand the language of the rich, but likewise to instruct the rich, that they may understand the language of the poor. At present, when they move among them, it is like moving among foreigners; and they ought to look upon their ignorance as a reproach, inasmuch as it would be far easier for them to master the dialect of their inferiors, than for the latter to master theirs. It is of course a minor consideration, though it ought not to be overlooked, that we should greatly improve our common language by this process.

Educated persons exploring among the dialects of the different counties of England might recover many a manly phrase and noble word, which time and a finical style of education have brought into desuetude. Our forefathers spoke a rough but vigorous language, brief and to the point. We have long ceased to imitate them in this. We deal in many words, avoid what is rude, abrupt, impetuous, and smooth down our style till it becomes afraid to rear its head above the ground. Like savage tribes, the poor, especially in the country, indulge in very figurative language, which, in spite of its great simplicity, is often eloquent. It is a duty, and ought to be a pleasure, to those who occupy the high places of society, to go down to these primitive strata of their mother-tongue, where they would find the solid basis which supports the vast superstructure, laid deep in the hearts and habits of the common people. If they did this, they would soon experience a pleasure in intercourse with their humbler countrymen, whom they would instruct, refine, and elevate by mingling with them. This would be by far the most effectual means of educating the people, and might possibly lead to conversations, to discussions, to a more enlarged social intercourse. The poor will feel the necessity of qualifying themselves for carrying on this intercourse agreeably; they will study, they will seek to polish their language and enlarge their conceptions, that they may be equal to the task of discoursing with educated men.

In the interchange of ideas and impressions, it appears to me that, although the poor may profit most, the rich also will benefit considerably; they will widen the sphere of their humanity, they will be able to carry into legislation more accurate notions of what is necessary to be done, they will soften their own hearts, improve their understandings, and correct their opinions of human nature by witnessing the display of those many excellent and noble qualities which are found, obscured by ignorance, and often side by side with coarseness and vulgarity, in the very lowest ranks of mankind.

However, to render practicable such an intermingling of classes, we must become a much less aristocratic people than we now are. Lord Robert Cecil, who has been in New Zealand and conversed with the savage natives, considers them far superior in intelligence to English peasants. This opinion is no doubt correct, for reasons which I have stated in another part of this work; but persons of education like Lord Robert are seldom able to measure exactly either the knowledge or the abilities of their

humbler countrymen. When they go abroad, the
aristocratic instincts which in England prevent their
mingling with the poor cease to operate, and they
are surprised to find among artisans and peasants
an amount of good sense and good manners which
they never noticed at home. The conclusions they
arrive at are partly erroneous, because the meanness
and poverty which everywhere characterize the ideas
of the ignorant are less visible in a foreign language.
Short-sighted persons half create the landscapes and
faces they admire. They perceive the outline and
a few salient points, and their imagination supplies
the rest. Nearly all minds become short-sighted
when they consider ideas, habits, and peculiarities
through the medium of a foreign language, and
under the influence of foreign climates. The things
we witness are at least new; and novelty often disguises from us their true character.

But in despotisms and semi-barbarous communities the lower orders are more on a level with the
upper, than under the sway of aristocratic institutions.
Where high and low are slaves, there is less reluctance in the former to cultivate familiarity with the
latter. In the Ottoman Empire for example, as well
as in France and Austria, the peasants are at once
gentler in their manners, and more intelligent in

conversation, than they are in England. The perpetual dread of punishment renders them submissive;
and their submissiveness induces their superiors to
converse with them. No apprehension is felt that
they will presume on any condescension that may be
shown them. In Switzerland, on the contrary, the
peasants are often rude and insolent, because they
are their own masters, and think themselves as good
as anybody else, though the diffusion of knowledge
is rapidly wearing away these asperities, and recon-
ciling freedom with politeness.

In many English counties the inhabitants are so
rough, so uncouth, so fierce, wild, and untractable,
that you might almost imagine yourself transported
back to the period when Angles, Jutes, and Danes
contended for the mastery. According to the testimony of judges and magistrates, the presence of the
schoolmaster is scarcely felt. The idioms in use are
nearly as old as the Heptarchy; and the manners
belong to the same period. But if you study the
countenances of the people, you soon become convinced that, whatever may be the exterior, there is a
store of good sense and shrewdness within. The eyes
are intelligent, the brow expansive and lofty, and the
expression about the mouth indicates a strange mixture of good-nature and ferocity, the former springing

from the condition of the mind, the latter resulting
from long-cherished habits.

With persons like these it is difficult to hold intercourse. Once, however, while travelling in Northumberland, I was shut up for several hours in a
railway carriage with some of these contemporaries
of Ella or Offa. The same number of Red Indians
would have been infinitely more quiet and gentle-
manly. Their language was scarcely English; their
looks and the tones of their voices were probably
those of their ancestors the Vikinger; but when I
began to converse with them they showed so much
good sense, good feeling, and kindliness of sentiment,
that I very soon forgot the queerness of their language and the roughness of their manners. Beyond
the necessities of their condition, they had perhaps
no ideas at all. Several of them had been in London,
which they regarded as a large trap, contrived to
catch countryfolk. All the while they remained in
it, they lived in terror; and right glad were they when
their business permitted them to return to their
wilds and mountains. They put me very much in
mind of an Arab chief whom I met at Cairo. He
had seldom been inside of a house, which he looked
upon with extreme suspicion, and entered with reluctance. While he was talking with me, a clock struck

behind his back. He started as if he had been shot, instantly put his hand on his sword, and turned round to face the unknown enemy. A Turk who happened to be present smiled, upon which the Arab, vexed at having exhibited tokens of alarm, observed proudly, " Had you been sitting in my tent, and heard suddenly behind you the whizzing of a spear, you would have started too."

My Northumbrian companions were used to clocks; but there were evidently circumstances in London life which astonished them quite as much as one of the measurers of time did the Bedouin.

It would take a great deal of intercourse, lecturing, reading, travelling, and experience, to transform such people into companions for educated men. Even the clergy, though thrown more than most other gentlemen among the humbler classes, run through the great mass of the population without mingling with it, like the waters of the Rhone through the Lake of Geneva.

The minds which have been disciplined by early education, which have been enlarged by great ideas, and sanctified, if I may so speak, by being made, like the Ark of the Covenant, the repository of mysterious and holy things, cannot, without much difficulty, be rendered intelligible to those minds which have en-

joyed no such advantages. The two great divisions
of the nation have distinct spheres of thought; and
the problem now to be solved is how to open up a
profitable communication between them. To accomplish this, we must find some middle point, towards
which the upper and lower classes may tend equally,
not so much by bringing down or raising their language and ideas, as by carefully studying each other.

I formerly knew the rector of a large parish, an
excellent man, full of apostolic zeal and charity,
whose ministry being attended by numbers of poor
persons, he determined to bring down his sermons to
their level. " I do not," he used to say, "preach at
all for you, or such as you; I address myself to the
humble and ignorant, who perhaps know nothing of
the Gospel but what they learn once a week from
me."   Well, did the congregation understand his
sermons?   On the contrary, knowing him to be a
great scholar, they persuaded themselves that his
sermons must necessarily be abstruse, and so never
tried to comprehend them, though they were models
of pure English, simple, beautiful, evangelical, equally
calculated to touch the heart and improve the mind.
In one respect, however, he did succeed; everybody
loved him, and his example was imitated, even while
his doctrine and reasoning were not properly under-

stood.   Objecting once to a Roman Catholic priest
against the use of Latin in the Mass-book, he replied
that the people understood it just as well as they
would have done had it been in French. " The things
spoken of," he said, " are beyond their reach; and it
is therefore immaterial in what language you address
them. The great point is to set them a good example. This I do as well as I can, and the poor
people appear to look up to me with affection. As
to ideas, dear creatures, they have none at all, and I
don't see how we are to give them any."   I talked
frequently with this good man's parishioners, and
found them thoroughly acquainted with the value of
sous and five-franc pieces, with the best modes of cultivating rye, flax, barley, oats, and even wheat;
but of most other things they knew as little as the
grooms of King Pepin.   Yet in France the priests go
a great deal among their parishioners, and talk with
them of all topics within their comprehension, and
often of some that are not exactly in that category.
This was particularly the case with my friend.   But
the harvest was not quite equal to his expectations;
and often, when he returned in the evening, he used
to talk jocularly of the difficulty he experienced in
getting any notions whatever into the minds of the
worthy peasants.

CHAPTER XIX.

USE OF THE ARTS IN EDUCATION.

Progress in Humanity.—Great Services of our Manufacturers.—Co-operation of the Nobility.—Private Collections of Statues and Pictures.—The Dukes of Wellington, Northumberland, and Devonshire.—The Poor in Italy.—Influence of Art.—Manchester Exhibition.—Comic Anecdotes.—State of the Ignorant at Exhibitions.—Populations turned into Stone.—Reading should precede Exhibitions.—Crystal Palace.—Monuments of Egypt ; of Italy.—The Revival.—The Awakening of Curiosity.—Benvenuto Cellini.—The Iliad.—'Hamlet.'—' Paradise Lost.'—The Life of Artists.—Scanty Knowledge of Art.—Real Object of Art.—Beauty.—Nature's Influence on the Soul.—Imitation.—The Sublime and Beautiful in Nature.—Sculptures and Paintings of Greece and Italy.—The Gallery of George IV.—'The Origin of the Milky Way.'—Rembrandt, Cuyp, Claude Lorraine.—Drawing.—The Athenians.—Taste of the Northern Nations.—High Intellects of England.

In real humanity we have perhaps made more progress during the last thirty years, than in any century and a half since the time of the Druids. All men now think, who think at all, of some new scheme for bettering the condition of the working classes. This is more especially the case among our opulent manufacturers, whose exertions and sacrifices in the cause of popular education deserve from the whole country the most grateful acknowledgments. They have held innumerable meetings; they have invented the half-time system; they have established schools, Lyceums, Institutes; they have built churches; they have endowed them; and they have brought together, in one grand Exhibition, an immense collection of great works of art, in the hope of improving the taste, and throwing open the well-springs of invention among the people.

In many of their undertakings they have been aided by the wealthy among the nobility, whose collections of works of art have been freely lent to aid the patriotic designs of the manufacturers. Rome, however, was not built in a day. It is a great point gained, that there exists among those who possess influence the desire to diffuse knowledge; the best mode of doing it will be discovered in time. Meanwhile it would greatly promote the object in view, if, all over the country, they who possess collections of statues, pictures, engraved gems, antiquities, or objects of elegant industry, were to throw them open, under proper restrictions, to the examination of their poorer neighbours. Several noblemen and gentlemen have already done this in part: the Duke of Northumber-

land, some years ago, threw open Northumberland
House to the public; the Duke of Wellington has
rendered Apsley House in some degree accessible; the
late Duke of Devonshire always admitted visitors
freely at Chatsworth; and many other distinguished
and opulent individuals have acted in like manner.

This is obviously one powerful means of imparting
instruction to the industrious classes. Half the knowledge possessed by the poor in Italy, Germany, and
many great cities of France is obtained in this way.
They visit galleries, and behold in ancient palaces
and churches the beautiful productions of genius, and
are in many instances excited to imitation. Where
this is not the case, they have their minds enlarged
and improved; they learn by degrees to respect the
creations of human intellect and industry, and are
thus allured into the track of civilization.

We are gradually falling into the same track,
though, owing to the vast size of London, the means
of education which exist are half lost. The British
Museum is no doubt well frequented; but the collection at the East India House and the treasures of
Marlborough House attract considerably less attention.
A beginning, however, has been made; and our artisans already recognize the utility of studying, in all
branches, the productions of other ages and countries.

This will facilitate the development of the national mind. All persons are fond of fine furniture, splendid vases, and exquisite bronzes; but in order to gratify their tastes at a reasonable price, our own workmen must be able to produce them. This they cannot do at present; but by studying the productions of other ages and countries, their ingenuity will be stimulated, and their taste improved.

The history of the great Manchester Exhibition of 1857 would no doubt furnish many comic illustrations of the ignorance of those who frequented it. Some few examples may be worth mentioning. A worthy operative from Oldham, or Oudham, as it is pronounced in Lancashire, after having sat gazing vacantly about for an hour and a half, at length inquired, of some one near, when the exhibition was to begin. It would be curious to know what this worthy Oudhamite expected; perhaps he thought there was to be a fight of two giants, or that some of the gentlemen and ladies on the wall would at length break silence, and give people a taste of their quality. One old woman, after some time seriously contemplating the ' Demoniac among the Tombs,' asked a person who stood by, if that was not Lord John Russell. Another of the Lancashire fair, having had her attention attracted to a curious coffer which had belonged to the Medici family, conceived herself to have made a discovery, and gravely assured one of her less enlightened friends that it was a medical chest.

When persons altogether uneducated find themselves suddenly thrown into the midst of a whole universe of art, they are completely stunned and bewildered. They are at a loss what to look at first. All their ideas are in mutiny. They do not know what to make of anything, but wander about in delightful uncertainty, in doubt whether they are really awake. The conclusions they arrive at in their own minds are of the strangest description. They resemble in some respects the Arabian traveller who, having passed through the ruins of some ancient city in which there were numerous statues, related that he had beheld a place whose inhabitants, having offended God by their wickedness, had all been turned into stone, and would remain in that state to the day of judgment.

If the owners of pictures and statues were generally to make them easy to be seen by the poor, there would be less wonder and more knowledge, the mind would be gradually prepared to encounter the great Exhibitions, such as that of 1851, of 1857 at Manchester, and the Crystal Palace. Still, in order that these things may produce their due effect, the taste

for reading should precede the visiting of Exhibitions;
otherwise people may gaze at some of the greatest
monuments of human genius without having any of
their faculties awakened, except those of wonder and
surprise. I have myself, in Egypt and Nubia, stood
before works of art, of which the real design and
history are lost for ever; and I find it impossible to
describe the yearning after discovery, and baffled
curiosity, I felt. The things, unquestionably, had a
meaning, perhaps a great and profound one; yet all
my care and study led only to conjecture.

It must be much the same with a majority of
visitors to the Crystal Palace. They know little or
nothing of Abousambal, Luxor, Karnak, Medinet
Habou, Denderah, Pompeii, or the Alhambra, of Mi-
chael Angelo or Bramante, of the Middle Ages or
the Revival; and therefore the lessons intended to be
taught by the collections of the Crystal Palace are
all but thrown away on them. I say all but thrown
away, because, if they inspire people with a wish to
know, they do serve one very useful purpose; that is,
the awakening of curiosity. In other words, the sight
of works of art creates the wish to read, while reading
diffuses a relish for works of art, and thus acting and
reacting, urge forward the national mind.

Show an ignorant man some piece of sculpture by

Benvenuto Cellini, he will probably admire its de-
licacy, its richness, its beauty; let him read the memoirs of that extraordinary artist, and his admiration
will be augmented a hundredfold.   In all other cases
a knowledge of the worker assists the appreciation of
his works.   From the biography of Homer, if we
had one, we should proceed with double zest to the
reading of the Iliad; and the biographies of Shakespeare and Milton form a pleasant avenue to ' Hamlet'
and ' Paradise Lost.'

Artists form a little world of themselves, and are
governed by motives and inducements springing from
their peculiar condition.   Oftentimes they labour
without reward; and their names are only then known,
when their owners are in the dust.   It is not true
that patronage, or even success, is necessary to call
forth the creative powers of the real artist, though
great genius, developed through art, is generally appreciated, because it exhibits itself in an enlightened
age.   Still it is by no means common, even among
the educated classes, to find persons who entertain
just notions of art.   The ordinary opinion is, that
whatever exists in nature may be the subject of artistic imitation, though, in truth, nothing deserves to
be imitated but what is calculated to benefit the
mind.   An old philosopher maintains that beauty

alone is the object of art; and his opinion may be much nearer the truth than appears at first sight. For if art does nothing but reproduce the ordinary objects around us, it leaves our minds very much where they were. The task which genius proposes to itself is the idealizing of what we behold, which is only to be done by investing everything with the beauty which, according to a complete theory of nature, belongs to it.

If it be beneficial to contemplate the productions of nature, if it soothes and invigorates to gaze at a summer sky, at a grand landscape, at the stars, at the ocean, it is scarcely less beneficial to study the imitations of those objects by man. The artist who undertakes to reproduce a landscape, suffers it by patient observation to pass into his soul, and then throws it forth again by a sort of reflection upon the canvass. The clouds, the many-coloured light, trees, rivers, mountains, castles, cathedrals, and cities start up before the eye just as they do in nature; but they have this advantage over the originals, that they can be conveyed to all parts of the earth, and be admired at all seasons. When everything outside a man's window is snow or sleet, fogs, mist, or rain-torrents, he may turn from the outer world, and behold, glowing along his walls, a series of summer

landscapes steeped in the richest colours of the South.
There alone, in fact, exist eternal sunshine and ver-
dure that never fades; and the effect of this department of art upon the soul is to enliven, to cheer,
to tranquillize, to elevate.

Strong natures find a joy analogous to their character in deserts, mountain torrents, cataracts, avalanches,
in forests shattered and uprooted by the hurricane.
The gentle seek relief in pastoral scenes, in green
glades, in umbrageous lakes, and calm rivers gliding
" at their own sweet will" through plains or valleys.

A higher pleasure is to be derived from grand and
beautiful representations of the human face divine.
Here the sources of interest are infinite,—history,
portraiture, illustrations of Scripture, embodiments of
the poets' ideas.   To walk through a gallery of well-
chosen statues and pictures is to have almost every
faculty of the soul awakened—above all, curiosity and
the wish to know.

Nothing, therefore, could possibly be happier than
the plan of throwing open, to the public of our large
towns, the great works of art contained in the private
galleries of England, by far the richest in the world.

It was formerly the distinction of a man sufficiently
opulent to pass beyond the Alps, to be acquainted with
the great productions of the Italian painters and the

masterpieces of Grecian sculpture; but by the system
which is now likely to be pursued, the English operative and labourer, with their wives and children, may
obtain a glimpse, at least, of that mighty world of art
rom which they have hitherto been excluded. This
I take to be an extraordinary privilege for the working
classes. The idea originated many years ago in London, when George IV. lent some of his finest pictures
to the Exhibition in Pall Mall. There the public, who
could never obtain admittance into palaces, might gaze
again and again upon the masterpiece of Tintoretto,
the Origin of the Milky Way, the Hippomenes and
Atalanta of Guido, the Jewish Rabbi of Rembrandt,
the Adoration of the Magi, by the same artist, with
landscapes of celestial beauty by Claude Lorraine, and
more terrestrial forms of the picturesque by Hobbima,
Ruysdael, and Cuyp.

The first step towards creating a taste for these
things is, by multiplying Schools of Design, to make
drawing an element in the education of all classes.
This was done by the most classical of classical nations,
the people of Athens, among whom, to draw was
almost as common as to read. Hence, in part at least,
that unerring taste by which they were distinguished
from the inhabitants of other cities, and that profusion
of sculpture which converted their ancient and sacred

citadel into a sort of terrestrial Olympus. There is no reason why what was done in other days and in other lands, should not again be done in England. Our taste, like the taste of all northern nations, differs in many respects from that of the Hellenic race, in which the sublime was always aimed at through extreme simplicity, whereas among us the way to it lies through vastness, through elevation, through the infinite multiplication and richness of details. The type of the imagination of the two races may be discovered in the Parthenon and in a Gothic cathedral: the one all grace, elegance, delicacy, and purity, reposing like a white lily in the sunshine of the South; the other, dark, gloomy, intricate, but full of grandeur, assimilating admirably with the storms, sleet, and cloudy atmosphere of Northern regions.

Let us cultivate our own idiosyncrasies. Nature has not been niggardly to us. Our country has produced men of the noblest stamp in every department of genius and intelligence; and in order at once to give proper amplitude to their renown, and call forth other men worthy to rank with them, we have only to awaken the faculties of the English people, which, so far as I am able to judge, are greatly superior to those of any contemporary nation.

The Bishop of Manchester is nevertheless right in

maintaining that, although knowledge may be more diffused in England than in France, the people of that country excel us in many tasteful manufactures. This is to be accounted for in two ways: first, the French operatives are more judiciously educated than ours; they do not know more, but what they do know is more to the purpose. We must not forget, however, that different nations appear to be adapted by nature to excel in different things. In England, from time immemorial, we have been in the habit of employing foreigners in certain branches of art and industry, as in architecture, sculpture, painting, and the chasing of silver and gold plate. Some foreign nations, as the Italians, Germans, and French, may perhaps surpass us by nature in certain branches of art, as the Greeks surpassed the Romans long after the education of the latter had embraced the same studies, and been carried as far as it could go.

As all men are not capable of all things, so neither are all nations. We find particular productions in every country, and it may possibly be a law of Providence, that every tribe and family of men should develope peculiar mental faculties. Education can only bring out what has been implanted by nature. When you cut and polish a precious stone, you only show the clouds and veins and colours it always contained, you add nothing to the sum of its qualities; so training, discipline, and education can only show you what the man is in himself. It only enables him to develope the powers of his intellect, but implants no new quality. What nature originally made him he will always continue—fit for some things, unfit for others. This fact will ensure the continuance of that universal dependence upon each other which constitutes the great bond of human society. We cultivate the friendship of other nations, because we stand in need of what they and their countries produce.

But these considerations should by no means lessen our desire to press forward the education of the people, since, until we shall have thoroughly explored our intellectual organization, and developed to the utmost the powers we possess, we cannot tell for what things, great or little, Nature has designed us.

CHAPTER XX.

THE STUDY OF LANGUAGES.

The Study of Languages.—Discouraged by Lord Stanley.—Our native Wealth of Thought.—Ancient Examples.—Power of the English Language.—Use of Foreign Tongues.—Dr. Booth.—The Working Men's College.—Examples of Self-taught Men.—Beneficial Influence of Languages.—Time the Measure of Study.—Foreign Literature. —Charles V.—Translation impossible.—Travelling without a Knowledge of Languages.—Anecdote of a Forty Years' Dunce.— Continental Workmen.—Teaching of Experience.—Mohammed Ali Pasha.—Cæsar and Sylla.—Foreign Customs and Manners.—French and German Classes.—Study of the East.—Conquests of the Solitary Student.—The Backwoods.—Delight of Learning.—The Honey of the Soul.

LORD Stanley, in his advice to the working classes, rather discourages them, than otherwise, from extending their attention to foreign languages. He observes, with truth, that there exists in English a body of thought and information sufficient to employ and quicken the intelligence of a great people. But there is no legislating for tastes and partialities. Lord Stanley, whose scholarship has not infected him with pedantry, was probably, when he gave utterance to the above opinion, thinking of the old Greeks, who usually contented themselves with the study of their own language. This however they did, not so much through the contempt of other tongues, as because they only, among the nations of those times, really possessed a literature. There was nothing to be learned but barren words by acquiring the dialects of their neighbours; and this, more than anything else, determined their practice.

We are placed in different circumstances. Our language, it is true, is equalled by no other now spoken among men, in richness, vigour, and poetical splendour. Yet it is only the expression of one people's intellect; and it may in many cases be useful for persons to learn the idioms of surrounding countries, that they may be able, as it were, to contemplate themselves from an external point of view.

Besides, of all acquisitions, that of modern languages is perhaps the easiest. Thus the young miner, who wrote an account of himself to the Dean of Hereford, had acquired before the age of twenty-two a reasonable knowledge of English grammar, French, and Latin, along with many other kinds of information. Again, Dr. Booth at Huddersfield, after distributing the prizes awarded to the students of 1857, in the Philosophical Hall, spoke of a youth, a namesake of his own, who, though he had to walk twelve miles every evening after work to study at the Mechanics' Institute, had made no little progress in French, music, and geometry. In Scotland it is by no means uncommon to find peasants who are acquainted with Latin, and in some cases with Greek also. Here in London, at the Working Men's College in Ormond Street, established by Professor Maurice, several of the students have applied themselves to modern languages, and some few to Greek and Latin, in which, it is said, they have made considerable proficiency.

I have myself known examples of men who, without any assistance at all from others, had learned French, Italian, Spanish, Greek, Latin, and several Oriental languages.

Though there be many other branches of knowledge to which popular students may usefully apply themselves, I would not therefore dissuade those from following their inclination who have taste for foreign languages. Nearly all men who have distinguished themselves in literature have possessed some slight tincture of classical learning. After the revival of letters, men attached too much importance to Greek and Latin; and upon this partiality we have bestowed the name of pedantry. Many now seem inclined to attach too little importance to the study of those languages, and too much to some other studies, which equally deserves to be regarded as pedantry. Montaigne's father was a pedant, who had his son taught Latin from the cradle, and had him awakened in the morning by the sounds of sweet music; but, with all his pedantry, he knew how to quicken the powers of genius, and his system, however ludicrous it may seem, gave a direction to the thoughts and studies of one of the ablest and most original of modern writers.* Too frequently, when we speak of the instruction proper to be imparted to the people, we seek to stamp upon it a sort of pauper impress, as if in the structure of their minds there were something essentially inferior to what is found in the upper classes. There need exist, however, no difference of education, except in degree. The man who possesses little time for study can never, in the extent of his acquirements, equal him who possesses much; and to maintain the contrary is only to throw dust in the eyes of the people.

Without in the least disparaging our own literature, it may yet be said that a knowledge of other literatures tends greatly to enlarge the mind. Everybody is familiar with Charles the Fifth's saying, that learn-

* See a masterly inquiry into Pierre Eyquem's plan of education in Mr. Bayle St. John's Life of Montaigne, i. 35–68.

ing a new language is like acquiring a new soul. There is certainly something strangely pleasing in mastering a foreign tongue, since it admits us into a new system of thoughts, manners, feelings, and opinions.

No one ever thoroughly understands a foreign nation without possessing its language. You might as easily translate a Frenchman into an Englishman as a French book into an English book. The information it contains may be given, you may state its arguments fairly, you may imitate the turns of thought; but the style, which is the essence of the book, is intransfusible. What rendered it French is completely lost, altogether apart from the mere words. The figures, the idioms, the collocations, the peculiar graces of one language can never be exactly represented by the forms of any other.

When a Greek author, for example, is sought to be rendered into French, all the majesty, power, and sweetness of the author evaporate in the process. The translation, of course, may possess some likeness to the original, as the reflection of a tree in water possesses a likeness to the tree; but there is this difference between them, that the one is alive, while the other is not. You feel, as you read the modern version, that there is something in the background which the words upon the page cannot impart to you. It is like standing in the street and listening to a speaker withindoors. You catch, perhaps, the general import of what is said, and follow, more or less, the strain of the reasoning; but the walls, the murmurs of the audience, the hum and bustle of life around you, intercept much that is requisite to form an exact conception of the beauty and persuasiveness of the whole. Every language, like every man, has its own features, which never can be imparted to any other.

To become painfully sensible of this, it is only necessary to pass into a strange country of which we know not the dialect. Remain there as long as you please, procure the ablest interpreters, and take all the other means in your power to become acquainted with the people and their manners, in spite of everything you will remain a stranger to the day of doom. But the moment you learn the language of the country, you feel that you have passed behind the veil, and know all that is to be known of them. Even their looks are clothed with additional meaning, and you walk about and feel yourself at home.

I knew a man in the East, who had lived there forty years without making the slightest progress towards mastering the language of the country. As a matter of course, he spoke of the inhabitants with great contempt, calling them stupid, morose, and detestable. He had in fact nothing in common with them. His manners, his ideas, his predilections were still in every respect French, and therefore the Orientals, who moved about him like so many actors on the stage, inspired him with no sympathy, and scarcely with any interest. He had married an Abyssinian wife, and, when he had anything very particular to say, spoke to her through an interpreter. How he managed to cure his patients—for he was a physician—is more than I can undertake to explain. He grew rich, however, kept a fine house and a large establishment, and, though he was turned seventy, talked of going back some day to France, and living there at his ease. He looked upon the natives only as creatures who could take physic and pay fees, but in every other point of view no better than so many puppets. Had he known how to converse with them, he might have filled his mind with extraordinary ideas, and gone back to Europe like a mirror reflecting the whole East.

Most people admit the advantages of travelling; but these advantages are beyond the reach of working men in general. The members of certain trades in Germany, France, and Spain, habitually devote several years of their youth to roving about their own country. They find little difficulty in getting work in the great towns and cities, and sometimes return to their native-places enriched not only with experience but with money. This is what they call seeing the world, and in a majority of instances they are supposed to be the better for it all their lives. They exhaust that restlessness which is the property of youth, and settle down contentedly to pursue their callings, marry a wife, and bring up a family.

Education, in the ordinary sense of the word, they often have none; but what education is intended to give they acquire by a different process. Mixing with all sorts of people, they immediately on leaving home find themselves, so to speak, in a state of warfare which cannot be carried on successfully without much courage, prudence, perseverance, and caution. The lesson is impressed upon their minds, that it is necessary to be polite towards strangers, and that, if they expect to be well treated, they must begin by treating others well.

The constant presence of poverty renders them economical, and economy leads to a rough sort of affluence. Instead of reading books they read men, study circumstances, calculate chances, compare different lines of conduct, and sometimes become able and sagacious men without knowing a single letter of the alphabet.

Mohammed Ali, Pasha of Egypt, could not read at forty years of age; many other great men have been in the same plight; but their minds were strong, their energy was indomitable, their singleness of purpose unswerving. They therefore overcame their ignorance, and ruled supremely over men infinitely more learned than themselves. Cæsar once said of Sylla he was ignorant of literature, and therefore could not be a dictator. This remark is more specious than wise. Jenghis Khan was ignorant of lite rature, and yet ruled over all Asia, not by hereditary right, but by the efforts of his own genius.

These observations are not intended to disparage any kind of knowledge, but only to keep in view this truth, that the mind may be stored in different ways.

Several classes of operatives, whose occupations render it impossible for them to travel, desire nevertheless to obtain some relish of foreign customs and manners. Of course they can read the narratives and descriptions of other Englishmen; but these only bring home a sort of pale copy of foreign lands, while learning the languages of those lands sets the learner down at once in the midst of the natives. He beholds their minds, if not their bodies, at work, discovers the mechanism of their thoughts, and perceives, or may perceive, every tint and shade in their manners, customs, ideas, morals, and habits.

I am aware that in several Mechanics' Institutes there are already French classes, and in some few German classes also. I am not offering suggestions therefore, but advocating the wider application of the existing practice. Some young men might perhaps like to devote themselves to Italian, or Spanish, or Turkish, or Arabic, or Persian. The East is coming nearer to us every day, and no man can foresee of what use the possession of such a language may some day prove to him. All difficulties melt away before the passionate love of knowledge. Whatever a man determines to know, he will know; I mean, if he confine his desires within the limits of what is possible to humanity. Men, by their firesides, in the country, without friends, without companions, with nothing to support them but the silent society of a book, have opened up for themselves an avenue to the delightful language of Hafiz and Firdousi, and found it practicable to wander in thought among the pillars of Chilminap, the cypress groves of Shiraz, and the mountain forests of Mazenderán.

If working men could be brought to think thus, they would certainly apply themselves at once to the subjugation of their ignorance. The task resembles, in some respects, settling in the Backwoods. When you alight from your waggon, with a wife and a host of children, you find yourself in the midst of a primeval wilderness, with nothing about you but trees, brakes, fens, in formidable luxuriance and extent. The first prospect is appalling, and you almost hesitate to apply the axe. But the mother of invention is at your elbow, you know you must have some place to house your family; down therefore falls one tree after another, the log-hut rises, the chimney smokes, the garden takes shape, and in the course of a short time corn waves over a fragment of the forest.

It is the same in learning : hour after hour does its work; difficulties diminish, pleasure augments, and the empty mind is by degrees filled with glorious furniture. Everything that is good for us is pleasant to learn. Many perhaps have been deterred from enriching their minds, by the saying of Aristotle, that the roots of the tree of knowledge are bitter, though the fruit is sweet. I think roots and all sweet; and perhaps the sweetest part of knowledge is the business of its acquisition. The bees do not appear to consider it a trouble to wander about in spring among the meadows, collecting honey from a thousand flowers. They inhale the perfume as they collect; and the hiving of their honey is not so sweet as the gathering of it.

Knowledge is sweeter than honey : it is, in fact, the honey of the soul; and of all delightful things, by far the most delightful is wandering over the intellectual world—over the past, over the present, over distant countries, over our own land—and gathering whatever is most beautiful in the thoughts and inventions of man.   How this labour can be considered irksome, I am at a loss to understand.   The only great obstacle appears to be to persuade men to pass the threshold ; for, that once accomplished, they will in general be unwilling to retreat.

CHAPTER XXI.

VIS INERTIÆ OF THE POOR.

Stubborn Resistance to Knowledge.—Montaigne.—Philosophy of
the Poor.—Repose of Society.—Result of Universal Instruction.—
Immorality of Ignorance.—Anecdote of a Little Boy and his
Father.—Depraved Neighbourhood.—Introduction of Schools.—
Changes produced by them.—Slow Diffusion of Knowledge in Ru-
ral Districts.—Itinerant Teachers.—Early Teaching obliterated.—
The Rev. F. Trench.—Rural Institutes.—Home Natural History.
—Aid of the Clergy.—Knowledge depends on Property.—Humble
Savings-Banks.—Anxieties of the Poor.—How to be lessened.—
Thinning the Population.—Colonial Natural History.—Settling in
India.—Useful and Imaginative Literature.

But though learning in itself be pleasant, it is impossible to conceal from ourselves that it is not always
easy to propagate this opinion among the poor. It is
a sort of infection which they will not take, just as
they will not take vaccination. They are told it will
do them good, but they are in doubt about it. By a
sort of pious stupidity, they persuade themselves that
it is setting God's laws at defiance; they will let
nature take its course; they will not set up their

wisdom against the wisdom of Providence; and they do not see that persons who have been vaccinated, and stuffed their heads with knowledge, are, after all, so very happy.

Montaigne observes that the poor have a sort of philosophy of their own, which often enables them to bear misfortunes better than the rich. When any affliction overtakes them, they say it was to be ; and they have, besides, comfortable euphemisms by which they conceal from themselves the formidable nature of the disasters that befall them. When the individuals they love are ill, they say they are poorly ; when they are in want, they say they are not so well off as they used to be ; when they die, they say they are gone to a better place. By this systematic extenuation, they blunt the sting of whatever happens to them.

In contemplating the great picture of society, we discover, intellectually speaking, its repose among the poor. There is little or no activity in their minds ; they go on, from generation to generation, in a sort of subdued contentment, listless, unambitious, unenterprising : finding themselves on the great level of humanity, they are satisfied to pick up what is before them, and remain there. You disturb this calm when you induce them to lift up their eyes and see to what knowledge may lead them.

It is no easy matter, however, to say beforehand what will be the result of the process in which we are engaged. So far as we can judge, to instruct the people is to render them more moral. ' Ignorance is unable to perceive the difference between two actions. It is a sort of mist, which confuses objects, and renders the mind uncertain respecting their forms and dimensions. The child who has knowledge often thinks more correctly about what is proper, and what is improper, becoming or unbecoming, than the parent who has been left to the sole teaching of experience. A very little boy, the pupil of a school set up by a friend of mine, hearing, one day, his father swearing furiously, said to him, " Oh, father, you should not use those bad words." The man, though rough and ignorant, was yet not without sensibility. He felt rebuked, and, taking up the little fellow in his arms, and kissing him with tears, said in a subdued voice, " You must not be too hard upon me, my boy; I never was at school, or taught the difference between right and wrong."

The neighbourhood to which this father and son belonged, is a low, depraved neighbourhood* in the

* In this part of London, however, very great efforts have been made, and are still making, to rescue all classes of the poor from ignorance, indigence, and vice. The humble institution called " The Cripple's Home and Refuge," in Hill-street, Dorset-square,

midst of a rich part of the town. When the schools were first set up, little else was visible in the streets than filth, rags, drunkenness in the parents, and squalor and disgusting habits among the children. At the instigation of the Rector, a lady whose name deserves to be remembered, though she is averse from making it public, gave at once five thousand pounds to build the schools, and set education in motion. I was present at the opening of them, though the lady was not, and heard the language of heartfelt gratitude in which many friends of the poor mentioned her goodness.

A great change soon took place in the whole neighbourhood; the children began to be better dressed, and in the morning you might see them in tens and twenties, with clean faces and hands, going towards the school. At length they increased to hundreds, and the streets once so infested with diminutive vagabonds, fighting, swearing, or wallowing in the filth, are now comparatively respectable and quiet.

deserves to be brought into public notice. It is divided into the Refuge, the Nursery, and the Cripple's Home. In the Refuge, girls who have lost their parents are received from ten to twenty, and taught to become useful servants; in the Nursery, infants from three weeks to two years old are taken care of from seven in the morning till seven in the evening, for threepence a day; in the Home, cripples, who have not lost their hands, are taught to earn their own living by various forms of industry.

The greatest difficulty, however, appears to be
encountered in the rural districts, where the inhabitants, being much scattered, can hardly by any contrivance have a school brought near them all; yet
little children cannot, even for the purposes of education, go far from their homes. To remedy this
evil, the only thing practicable is, to create a class
of itinerant schoolmasters and schoolmistresses, who
might be appointed to a circuit, and give instruction,
in hamlets too small to have a school of their own,
on certain days of the week. This plan might be
made to fall in with that of the Dean of Hereford,
who has suggested the practicability of extending the
half-time system to the agricultural parts of the
country.

When this question was discussed at a meeting
in Basingstoke, certain individuals representing the
farming interest ridiculed the idea of an alternate
ploughboy, which they denounced as altogether
visionary. But, in reply, it was observed by the
advocates of education, that when the cultivators of
the soil come to understand what is best for themselves, they will urge no objection against any reasonable means of imparting knowledge to the working
classes. In agriculture, as in everything else, the
skilled labourer is infinitely more valuable than the

dunce, because there is no form of industry in which intelligence and activity of mind are not needed. Besides, the force of civilization is not to be resisted even by the sturdiest farmers; if the rest of the community determine that knowledge shall be generally diffused, it will not be possible for the less instructed classes to offer any permanent resistance to their will.

Experience, however, shows that, even when labouring men have been taught to read in their childhood, the toil and drudgery, to which they are afterwards obliged to devote themselves, frequently obliterate from their memories nearly all traces of their early acquirements. The Rev. F. Trench found, in the hospital at Reading, a number of poor men totally unable to solace themselves, during their illness, with the Bible or any other book, though when boys they had been taught both to read and write. They had been acted upon by no inducement to keep up the humble knowledge they had gained : they had access to no lending-libraries; and the book-hawker was not then in existence to bring Milton, Bunyan, and De Foe to their firesides.

All the pains that can be taken by the enlightened and benevolent will yet, perhaps, always leave some unfortunate individuals, scattered here and there through the secluded parts of the country, unvisited by the light of knowledge, though very much may be done by setting up in the agricultural counties establishments analogous to Mechanics' Institutes. If these were judiciously located in the small towns and considerable villages, and furnished with a room for the supply of ordinary refreshments, the labourers would no doubt resort to them. At first their reading would be slight and desultory; but though it might be difficult, it would certainly not be impossible to interest them by degrees. Books like White's 'Natural History of Selborne' might be found to have a charm for many, because they would reveal to them what abundant sources of pleasure and instruction lie around us everywhere. In the fens and marshes, their attention might be directed to the habits of aquatic birds, and to the natural history of such plants as abound in swampy lands. In hilly or mountainous districts, their minds might be stored by information respecting the rocks, minerals, and medicinal springs appertaining to such localities.

The clergy, nearly all over the kingdom, have shown a willingness to co-operate with the schoolmaster in imparting civilization to the poor. They would therefore often visit these establishments, and, in familiar lectures adapted to the understandings

of their hearers, would point out and explain everything in the vicinity calculated to strike their imaginations and awaken curiosity. The working classes
can never become antiquaries; but they would listen
with pleasure to accounts of the ruins of ancient
abbeys or castles, especially if good drawings of the
objects under consideration were exhibited to them.
The same thing may be said of natural history. In
general the poor notice little of the natural productions or historical monuments of the counties in which
they live. Absorbed by ideas of their daily wants,
they can seldom be induced to bring their minds to
bear steadily on anything else. To give them a taste
for knowledge, therefore, it is necessary to diminish
that devouring solicitude which uncertainty about the
means of subsistence inevitably creates.

This has been attempted, in various parts of the
country, by the setting up of small Savings Banks,
and societies for the acquisition of plots of land.
That excellent man the Dean of Hereford has
actively encouraged, within his deanery, everything
which has a tendency to better the condition of the
poor; and several gentlemen in the neighbourhood of
the city have willingly co-operated with him. This
they have done from the conviction that the first
step towards educating the people is to improve their

physical condition. Enable a man to become master of a little property, and it will not be difficult to imbue him with knowledge, or at least to inoculate him with the wish to educate his children.

When men are at ease about their daily bread, they will attend to lectures, and experience an interest in the objects around them. The labourer whose cupboard is empty, whose children are hungry, whose wife is tattered and emaciated, will not regard with very eager curiosity drawings of beasts or birds, or of the most magnificent cathedral or aspiring castle that ever frowned over a feudal landscape. This fact grandees are apt to forget while speculating on the destinies of the working classes. They talk of what may be done in so many hours, not considering that many, perhaps most of those hours must be consumed in contriving how to keep body and soul together. They may have plenty of time at their disposal; but that with them is just the obstacle to all study. Instead of poring over diagrams, they are meditating upon their relations to the baker and butcher, and wondering, perhaps, how long their patience will hold out. To free their minds from these cankering cares is the first step towards giving them a taste for education. It would, of course, be useless to imagine the existence of a Utopia in England, in which everybody would be engaged in thinking of his neighbour; but it is not unreasonable to demand of those who profess an earnest wish to benefit the poor, to begin their operations by doing all that may be found practicable towards securing to them the means of subsistence. The most practicable method of accomplishing this would be to multiply Schools of Emigration, by which the surplus labour of this country might be regularly transferred to other provinces of the empire, in which it would find sure and adequate remuneration. The advocates of high wages at home may easily convince themselves, if they please, that they are only to be attained by diminishing the number of competitors for labour. Obviously, when there is much to do, and when there are few to do it, employers will be constrained to raise wages. It would be well, therefore, for the humbler classes, if the supply of labour could always be made to fall somewhat short of the demand, which may without difficulty be done by facilitating the exodus of the population.

Even in ordinary schools and rural Institutes, it would be well to impart to the people some information respecting our outlying possessions and dependencies, in which several of the most beautiful productions of nature are found. Masses of gold from Australia, of ivory from Africa, skins of the rhinoceros, hippopotamus, and antelope, with drawings of rare

trees, plants, and shrubs, such as the cinnamon from
Ceylon, the tea-tree from Assam, the coffee-tree from
the Mauritius, might be exhibited to the learners.
At the same time it would be easy to convey to them
a tolerably clear idea of the cultivation of indigo,
opium, and cotton, which would be likely to excite in
their minds the wish to settle in India, where they
would by degrees constitute the strength and security
of our Asiatic empire.

But upon the nature and extent of instruction to be
imparted in these schools and institutes, the clergy
will themselves be able to decide. They must take
care, however, not to aim exclusively at mere utility.
The minds of the poor, as well as those of other classes,
require to be occasionally refreshed by the dews of
imaginative literature, without which everything you
plant in them will be stunted and wither away. It is,
no doubt, good for a working man to be acquainted
with the steam-engine, which in all likelihood will soon
be beheld superseding, in our fields, the horse, the ox,
the scythe, and the sickle. But he cannot be always
thinking of pistons and boilers. His mind will occasionally long to put on the wings of fancy, and sweep
joyously over the perfumed plains of Araby and Ind.
From these excursions it will return refreshed and
invigorated, to encounter the less pleasing toils of
everyday life.

CHAPTER XXII.

EFFECTS OF THE DIFFUSION OF KNOWLEDGE.

Strange Discussions.—Apprehensions of Parliament.—Tameness of Ignorance.—Multiplication of Schools.—The Secular System.— Fruit of Knowledge.—Good and Bad Laws.—Amelioration of the Legislature.—Education, a Political Power.—Idea of God.—The Earth and its Inhabitants.—Reward of Labour.—Too Much and Too Little.—Study of Our Social System.—Knowledge regarded too much as a Plaything.—Light Literature.—Fiction, Music, and the Drama.—Recreations of Various Classes.—Just remark of the 'Times.'—Vulgar Adages.—Riches of the Earth.—The Mind's Possessions.—Limits of the Human Faculties.—Ancient Nations. —Crowded Population.—The Hostilities of Life.—Religious Sentiment.

SOME writers and speakers on Education are anxious to ascertain whether or not it would be expedient to give the people unlimited knowledge. This is very much like inquiring whether, when a man experiences much difficulty in getting a few shillings to buy bread, it would or would not be expedient that he should have ten thousand a year.

Strange as it may seem, there really does exist in the British Parliament a strong apprehension of the results of imparting knowledge to the people. It beholds them patient and obedient in ignorance, but is not quite so sure that they will be obedient when they possess enlightenment. Other legislators call to mind their classical reading—

"Mens agitat molem, et magno se corpore miscet,"

and fear that, when the mind begins to agitate the mass, it may become turbulent and ungovernable. These ideas, however, they keep in the background. They seek to hold in check the popular enthusiasm for education, under pretence of respecting the orders of the Privy Council, which, according to them, multiplies schools fast enough. But what they profess to dread is the secular system, though what they mean by the expression it is difficult to understand, unless they allude to political instruction.

Before imparting knowledge to the people, governments should certainly inquire what is likely to be the result. The more men know, the stronger will become their appetite for enjoyment, intellectual and physical. Therefore, if you augment their appetite, you must think seriously of augmenting their means of satisfying it. Men soon learn that all enjoyments are purchased by property, that property is acquired by industry, that industry is fostered by good laws, and obstructed by bad ones, that laws good and bad are enacted by Parliament, that Parliament enacts bad laws because they who sit in it do not understand the interests of the people, and that consequently, in order to secure to the people all the advantages which they ought to derive from civil government, Parliament must be so organized as to make it equal to the wants of the empire.

Thus education is obviously shown to be a political power, and as such it must be dealt with. Ignorance is tame because it does not know how to help itself; upon ignorance, therefore, all misgovernment is based, though not upon ignorance alone. Some kinds of knowledge are very compatible with despotism,—knowledge of science, knowledge of the fine arts, and so on. It is moral, religious, and political knowledge that renders men difficult to be misgoverned.

The idea of God is the great point upon which all human liberty turns. If you could take away this, you might plunge the whole world into absolute servitude. It is the only foundation upon which our theories of justice, equality of rights, and freedom can possibly repose. I do not say that a well-instructed people would be turbulent, clamorous, mutinous, and idle. Quite the reverse. The more a man knows of the necessary conditions of humanity, the more deep becomes his conviction that everybody

must or should work. He contemplates the earth
and its inhabitants; and the discovery is forced upon
him that the latter, by the irresistible laws of their
nature, are compelled to derive their sustenance from
the former. The earth is capable of sustaining its
children; but it conceals its gifts, and places them
under the necessity of asking and seeking for what
they need. But when they perform the work, they
ought clearly to obtain the results. So much labour
deserves so much advantage.

This suggests the idea that, when the industrious
classes are unable to subsist properly by their industry,
public affairs must inevitably be mismanaged. Not
at all, perhaps, in the ordinary sense. The Ministers
of the day may perhaps do all they can to square the
national income and expenditure, and therefore they
are not to blame. The impediment to the proper
working of society lies in the internal structure of
society itself. Something has got wrong there. There
is some obstruction; the nutritive juices of the body
politic are not properly diffused; too much gets into
some members, and produces corruption, too little into
others, and produces leanness, withering, and decay of
strength.

The truth then makes itself manifest, that the
whole social machine requires to be examined, in

order that its forces may be directed as they ought, and its whole action brought into harmony. A well-instructed people would soon become acquainted with these facts, and order their own movements accordingly. Even they, however, might blunder at first in searching after the necessary remedy, but they would persevere in their investigations until they got at the truth.

At present the people of this country, though supposed to be serious and plodding, are inclined to look upon knowledge rather as a plaything, than as a mighty instrument for improving the condition of society. No doubt there are numerous exceptions; but a majority of all classes, learned and unlearned, rich and poor, are more on the look-out for amusement than for anything else. There are those who believe that light and pleasing literature, such as excites the fancy and the imagination, would serve as a sort of pioneer to sound and useful knowledge, that fiction will prepare the way for fact, that minds intoxicated by descriptions of an ideal world will be the best qualified to struggle with realities.

This, however, is hardly reconcilable with experience. Well-directed studies doubtless include amusement. A man cannot be always serious, always reflecting, always at work. He must laugh some-

times, relax sometimes, be entertained sometimes.
Consequently music, reading fictions, and dramatic
exhibitions lie within the scope of popular education.
But none of all these things should be allowed to
take the lead. They should be properly subordinated
to the employment of the mind, which is to discover
the best means of promoting the welfare of the individual, and of society.

The health of the body requires that sedentary
persons should take exercise, that they who habitually labour, which to them is exercise, should enjoy
intervals of repose. It is so, obviously, with the mind.
Intense intellectual toil, protracted indefinitely without intervals of relaxation, would, in all but the most
powerful minds, soon terminate in a paralysis of the
faculties.

The ' Times ' remarks very justly that many persons expect a great deal too much of education, just
as in old times too much was expected of philosophy. But this observation may suggest false ideas.
The ancients did not begin to talk of philosophy as
a panacea for all the ills that flesh is heir to, until
they had ceased to possess any true philosophy at
all. When philosophy was a real living power, the
extent of its influence was better understood. People knew what it could, and what it could not do.

We should in like manner seek to comprehend the true mission of education. There is often a great deal of wisdom in vulgar adages, which we ought not to reject on account of the form in which they come to us. We may therefore profitably bear in mind that education is not a power which can make a silk purse out of a sow's ear. The instincts, the faculties, the powers which it finds in a man, it can bring out, but it can create nothing. It is in fact only the light which shows a man his internal possessions.

The education of the whole human race, to some extent, does the same for its common possession, the material world. It has enabled us to extract from the earth gold and silver, copper and steel, and coal, and many other metals and minerals, in addition to the food upon which we daily subsist. But mankind reach a high degree of material civilization before they think of properly developing the possessions of the mind. When we behold a vast multitude, and reflect upon what we see, we cannot avoid lamenting that so much intellectual power as lies latent in it, should be suffered to remain altogether unproductive. But, because we know not what men are, we must not jump to the conclusion that education can make them what it pleases. The measure of every man's faculties is fixed by nature, so that no art or contrivance can possibly enlarge his intellectual domains. You might as well attempt by culture to convert an elm into an oak, as to make a man not gifted with imagination into a poet. When we reach the boundaries of our mental powers, we may chafe against them, we may rail against nature, we may dissemble our weakness, but we must stop. The same Power which said to the ocean, " Hitherto shalt thou come, and no further," has said the same thing to the human mind.

But very few, if any, have ever thoroughly unfolded the map of their own souls. They do not know what they are, or how much faculty they possess. Very often, instead of pushing their self-discoveries, they sit down like the old geographers, and write upon the margin of their minds, "All beyond this is barren desert or pathless wilderness." Because they are too indolent to proceed any further, they easily persuade themselves that no sources of pleasure or profit remain unvisited. As no one, perhaps, ever made the most of himself, people have easily been betrayed into the belief that the mind is really infinite; not knowing where it ends, they imagine it has no end.

There are, of course, many ways in which education may be contemplated, and the world is too apt to regard it merely as a means of self-aggrandisement.

Several ancient nations took the opposite point of view, and dwelt chiefly, if not exclusively, on the internal satisfaction it was calculated to impart. They thought it sordid to make a traffic of the riches of the soul. Happiness, they contended, is what we are in search of; and this is not secured by the amplitude of our external possessions, but by the discipline and condition of our own minds. What a man has within his soul, he cannot be deprived of by other men, unless they take his life. He can sit in darkness, and flood the whole image of the universe with light, because he has it in his mind, and can do what he pleases with whatever is there.

This however they carried much too far; and the wisest of them taught that health, a moderate competence, and freedom are necessary to happiness. For those, consequently, who have neither health, competence, nor freedom, education is the instrument by which they are to acquire all three. In most cases, he who knows how to practise the rules of prudence enjoys good health. In these days of competition and a crowded population, a competence is less easy to be acquired; and still further beyond the reach of individual exertion lies liberty.

It follows that a man, who in these days sets about acquiring knowledge, must regard himself as entering upon a system of perpetual warfare. He has first to subdue his own indolence and inaptitude for study, his own prejudices, his own passions, his own leanings towards dissipation and vice; in the next place, he has to overcome the prejudices and misapprehensions of others, that they may permit him to secure for himself the means of maintaining himself and his family; and then he has to co-operate with millions in acquiring or enlarging the inestimable possession of civil liberty.

To me it seems quite clear that he never will or can do this without being supported by a powerful religious sentiment, suggesting, and perpetually keeping alive, the conviction that he is not strong in his own strength, but that there is an all-powerful arm at his back, ready to support him in every trial, to give efficacy to his virtuous exertions, and to bless him with that sunshine of the heart which renders a man absolutely invincible in the battle of life.

CHAPTER XXIII.

STUDY OF THE SOCIAL SCIENCES.

National Association.—Lord Brougham.—Lord Stanley.—Anecdote of Extraordinary Success.—On what based.—Studies of Men of Business.—The Gifts of Nature.—The Schoolmaster may teach their Use.— Study of Jurisprudence.—The Social Influence of Laws. —Causes of Plenty or Famine.—Legal Reforms.—Preliminaries to the Study of the Law.—Abolition of Crafts and Mysteries.—Our Legal Institutions still unapproachable to the People. — Professional Patois. — Useless Terminologies. — Sir John Pakington the Advocate of Universal Knowledge.—Cures of Hunger, Thirst, and Ignorance.—Familiar Dialectics.—History and Science of Education.—Lord John Russell maintains that the Profession of a Teacher is honourable.—No large Theory of Education.—Diversities of Opinion in the Legislature.—The proper Business of Education. Freedom an Affair of Race.—The Ancient Saxons.

I HAVE already, in an early part of this work, touched slightly upon those branches of knowledge which are now beginning to be called the Social Sciences. Until very recently, their importance to the people was not generally acknowledged; but we have now at length witnessed the establishment of an Association, the aim of which is to attract public attention to these subjects. Lord Brougham, who has always advocated the diffusion of knowledge, and has himself done great service to the cause of education, has again come forward and placed himself at the head of the movement, in company with Lord John Russell, Sir John Pakington, Lord Stanley, and several other gentlemen.

We may consequently hope that numbers among the people, who have hitherto made little or no exertion to improve their own minds, will be urged to adopt a new course. In order to rouse their mental activity, the founders of the Association addressed themselves to some of their strongest feelings. Lord Stanley, both at Wigan and Birmingham, related an anecdote illustrating the way in which, even in this old and crowded country, knowledge, ability, and good conduct sometimes enable men to enrich themselves. Three individuals, he said, who not many years ago subsisted on wages of a few shillings a week, were now each receiving, from one Firm, a salary equal to that of an Under-Secretary of State, that is, fifteen hundred a year.

So great a degree of success could, obviously, not be attained without considerable knowledge; but what kind of knowledge? Lord Stanley should have conversed with those gentlemen, in order, if possible, to discover how they had qualified themselves to earn their immense salaries. He would have found, I think, that they had not habitually suffered their minds to wander into the pleasant paths of study, but had, as a rule, confined them within the circle of those things which belong to the practice of business. Every man should endeavour to understand what he wants in this world. That knowledge will greatly assist him in determining what he ought to study, and what he ought to do. If his object be to found a family and enrich it, he should obviously seek to master all the processes which contribute to the generation of wealth. These, I feel sure, were the things mainly, if not exclusively, attended to by Lord Stanley's triumvirate. They found out the secret how to make capital breed capital, and were wisely permitted by their employers to share the opulence they knew how to create.

But perhaps, if we investigate the matter thoroughly, it may appear that men of this class are more indebted to nature than to the schoolmaster. Mind, organization, intellect—call it what you will—is inbreathed with our souls. It is a pearl of great price, which comes to us without our seeking. We may bring it forth, we may blanch, we may polish it, we may set it off to advantage, we may take it to the proper market; but that is all we can do. The thing is not of our creating. God gave it to us when he gave us the breath of life; but undoubtedly it is in our power to wrap the talent intrusted to us in a napkin, and hide it from the sight of men, or to turn it actively to account.

The study of the social sciences is the best means in our power of developing the useful qualities we may happen to possess. These sciences are various; but among them it may be doubted whether there be one more important than a knowledge of the laws, a department of study over which Lord John Russell has been very properly selected to preside. There is no hearth, however humble, to which the influence of these laws does not extend: it is like the very air we breathe: it is in fact the air of our political life; upon it depends our happiness or our misery, our elevation in the social scale to the greatest heights of civilization, or our degradation to the depths of barbarism. History teaches us no truth more constantly or plainly than this. With the amelioration of the laws, spring up plenty and contentment, public spirit, the love of country, learning, a taste for the arts, industry, commerce, internal peace, with all the affections and charities of domestic life. By bad laws brother is set against brother, husband against wife. By the same agency the peasant's bread is taken from his lips, and famine set to rock the cradle of his children.   Where good law is, there is scarcely anything wanting.   It is in fact the power by which every man is enabled to obtain his own, to keep his own, and to turn everything he possesses—mental, moral, or bodily—to the best possible account for himself and his family.

No man, perhaps, knows this better than Lord Brougham; and therefore it is not surprising he should insist upon what has been done during the last quarter of a century, in part through his own praiseworthy exertions, for the improvement of the laws of this country.   Still it appears extremely difficult to bring to bear the attention of the public generally upon a subject so abstruse and difficult as our laws.   No doubt they might be so simplified and explained as to be intelligible to popular students. But the first step towards this would be the abandonment of that peculiar terminology which lawyers persist in making use of, so that to obtain even a glimpse of their meaning we often need to have their language translated into the vernacular.

It is the tendency of civilization to destroy all crafts and mysteries, to lead the public into the sanctuaries of professions, to abolish exclusive studies, and render the possessors of all kinds of knowledge eager to share what inquiry has taught them, with the people. Very little, however, has hitherto been done towards rendering easy our entrance into the temple of law. Heaven only knows what toil would even now be necessary, to take up the thread of our legal history from the settlement of the Jutes in Kent, and follow it down, step by step, to the establishment of the National Association at Birmingham.

Every profession has its patois, which none but the natives perfectly understand. If you live among them, you acquire by degrees familiarity with some few phrases, so as to be able to keep up friendly intercourse. But you are never thoroughly initiated, and, every day of your life, hear sounds uttered around you to which you can attach no meaning. This is the fault of the professions themselves, not of the public. In a civilized community there should be as few jargons as possible. Every educated man ought to be able to understand every other educated man, even when speaking of the business of his profession. All technical terms, not absolutely necessary to ensure clearness of expression, ought to be given up at once. Instead of this, we observe around us a growing tendency to introduce new words, even while we are labouring to deliver ourselves from the multitude of useless terms which already beset us.

Sir John Pakington has completely identified himself with the subject of education, insomuch that, whenever the word is pronounced, his name is irresistibly suggested. In the National Association this department, therefore, has been very properly appropriated to him ; and from the earnestness and vigour of his character, we may safely infer that he will do all that can be done towards investing it with popular interest. But Sir John Pakington is not a flatterer of the people. Whenever the extent and variety of their ignorance are in question, he is not mealy-mouthed. He is the physician who says to the patient, " You are in a very bad state ; you are afflicted by more than one disease, and your complaints are inveterate. Nevertheless, if you follow my directions, I will cure you."

Above the doors of many country inns in France, we find written the following words,—" Hunger and thirst cured here ;" and Montaigne, who probably had often beheld that inscription, observes, in his Essays, that eating is the cure of hunger. So, according to Sir John Pakington, education is the cure of ignorance. It is no easy matter, however, to get people to take this physic. They who make the trial find it considerably more difficult than the task of the French innkeepers. When people are hungry and thirsty, they are seldom reluctant to take the proper remedies; but when the soul is athirst, they who have the care of it will often let it dwindle away and pine a long time, before they take a single step towards satisfying it. We have no history of education; otherwise we should perhaps discover that the infiltration of ideas into the popular mind has always been an arduous enterprise. In many countries, a good deal more use has been made of the tongue than of books, not so much in the way of lectures, as in that of familiar dialectics. Even with children this method, when it can be followed, is always the best. By pursuing it you make them find out that they want something, that they don't know what it is, but that by talking with you they may possibly make the discovery; you pique their curiosity, you impart activity to their pride, you pit their emulation against the emulation of their companions; you teach them to dispute, and set them disputing with each other; and the result generally is a strong desire of investigation.

It is hardly too much to say, that up to this time we know very little of education as a science. Hardly any one thinks himself too ignorant to educate others; antiquated excisemen, grooms, cooks, butlers, set up schools, and undertake to enlighten the rising gene-

ration. Their domain, however, has already been in-
vaded by trained schoolmasters and schoolmistresses,
whose numbers are daily augmenting, so that they
will soon become formidable to the undisciplined
pedagogues. But we are not yet on the right track.
Lord John Russell once said in Parliament, that the
way to get good teachers was to connect the idea of
honour with the profession of teaching. Hitherto,
however, very little has been done towards reaching
this consummation. No lofty or comprehensive theory
of education prevails among us. When the subject is
brought before Parliament, we find that, among its
members, there are almost as many theories as individuals. Scarcely any two are agreed as to what it
is desirable to teach the people, or respecting the
method of teaching it. Some are even found to
maintain that, in order to reach the highest destiny of
man, ignorance is perhaps after all the best guide.

Such could never be the case, were we accustomed
to regard education from a scientific point of view.
We should then perceive that in itself it is simply
a method, a discipline, a mode of awakening and
training the faculties of the mind. It does not interfere with the nature of the things that are introduced
into the mind, it does not meddle with truth or false-
hood, it does not inculcate this, or denounce that; it

only shows men the way in which they ought to make use of their intellectual, moral, and physical powers.

In common parlance, education no doubt is often used as a synonym of knowledge, the means being confounded with the end. But, in whatever light we view it, we can scarcely refuse to acknowledge that we are very much at sea in reference to its power and object. Sir John Pakington has frequently made allusion to a fact, which ought to re-assure those who apprehend political inconveniences from the spread of education. In many despotic countries, very great pains are taken to diffuse knowledge among the people, because no fear is entertained that it will render them seditious or unruly. Freedom is more an affair of race than of cultivation.

The ancient Saxons, from whom we are descended, were so jealous of authority, that in time of peace they refused to recognize any supreme chief. When a war broke out, they chose by lot some one from among their nobles to carry it on; but with the cessation of hostilities his superior command ceased, and he descended again to the common level of his peers. This feeling had not been cherished in the ancient Saxons by education. They could neither read nor write; they worshipped Thor and Woden, and per-

STUDY OF THE SOCIAL SCIENCES.   289

haps thought the Elbe and the Rhine the only great rivers in the world. But they had imbibed from their fathers and mothers the belief that life without liberty was of no value at all; and therefore it was that they could endure nothing in the shape of a tyrant. If knowledge could ensure freedom, there is no population in modern Europe which would not be freer than the ancient Saxons; and yet there are very few half so free. No social revolutions need, consequently, be anticipated from the action of the schoolmaster.

CHAPTER XXIV.

THE SOCIAL SCIENCES (CONTINUED).

Difficulty of Distributing Knowledge.—How to ensure the Co-operation of the Poor.—Laws of Health.—National Association Migra-
tory.—Important Advantages of this.—Example of Lord Stanley.—
Disagreeable but useful Studies.—Everybody's Business.—Force
of Public Opinion.—Chronicles of Plagues and Pestilences.—How
caused.—Health in Ancient and Modern Capitals, Thebes, Babylon,
Athens, Rome; Cities of France and Germany.—Errors of Reformers.—Pre-eminence of London as a Habitation for Man.—
Subterranean Architecture.—Pestilential Effluvia.—Hovels of the
Poor.—First Step towards Improvement.—Contrast between the
Dwellings of Rich and Poor.—Knowledge and Squalor incom-
patible.—Shortcomings of Parliament.—Museum of Cottage Architecture.—Cottage Gardens, Bees and Flowers.—Right of Common.
—Swift.—Mission of Education.

THEY are no doubt correct who maintain that there
is no lack of knowledge in the world, and that all
we now need is to distribute it. The business of
distribution, however, is far from being an easy one.
Almost from the remotest ages, there have existed
a few individuals who possessed all the theory of
civilization, that is, who comprehended in the largest

sense, the wants of society, and the means of supplying them. The difficulty has always been, to cause knowledge to infiltrate, so to speak, through the vast masses of mankind, so as to moisten and render them fit to be moulded into the proper forms by political philosophy.

The Association for the Promotion of Social Science has been established in order to diffuse, through the great body of the English people, several kinds of knowledge already in existence. To operate upon the poor for their own good, it is necessary that the poor should themselves understand what is done for them, and why it is done. They might otherwise completely counteract their benefactors. In the matter of health, for example, it would be of little avail to direct people what to do for the purpose of preserving it, if, when they had heard the directions, they were to go and do the contrary. To ensure their co-operation, you must make them understand that they will derive great benefit from it, and also how they will derive it.

When you inform a labouring man that the following of certain sanitary rules will be beneficial to him, he may believe you upon your word. But that is not enough. To place him in a proper situation, you must show him distinctly that, by acting in conformity with your system, he will be sure to promote his own and his family's health, and that health is money, and that money, in conjunction with many comforts, will procure him leisure, that leisure will enable him to acquire more knowledge, and that this again will be an additional source of wealth and prosperity.

These truths were stated in a very striking manner by Lord Palmerston, in a speech delivered at Manchester in 1856. " If a man were to enter a town of some foreign country, where there were laws, the violation of which was attended with pain, imprisonment, or it may be with death, would he not be deemed mad, if he did not take the earliest opportunity to make himself acquainted with those enactments, so that he might avoid the penalties attached to their infringement? Yet there are laws of nature, applicable to the daily pursuits of men, which, if not attended to, inflict bodily pain in the form of disease, imprisonment in the shape of the loss of corporeal powers, and even death through the neglect of those sanitary conditions on which life depends. How important then it is, that the working classes should be made aware of those natural laws and regulations which are indispensable to their own welfare, and to that of their families."

To bring about these results, the Association will hold its meetings in different parts of the kingdom, and its transactions will be made known by the journals to hundreds of thousands who are not present at the reading of its papers. The opinions of its members will be discussed, adopted, or controverted; fresh inquiries will be set on foot, statistics will be examined, and, in the end, the attention of the whole community may be attracted to the subject.

Lord Stanley, who is placed at the head of the sanitary department, has so active and vigorous a mind, and is so earnest in his desire to promote the public good, that he cannot fail to excite considerable emulation among persons of his own class, as well as to awaken curiosity among those who are chiefly interested in the inquiry. To improve the society in which we live, we must often consent to lay aside our elegant and lofty studies, and enter upon the consideration of topics revolting and almost loathsome in themselves. From the splendour and magnificence of our great cities, we must for a while avert our eyes, and plunge into that subterranean system of drains, arches, pipes, and sewers by which the most superb structures above-ground are rendered habitable.

At first sight it may appear unnecessary for persons in general to concern themselves about such things.

It is not their business, it may be said, to meddle with sewers; and therefore why should they trouble themselves with the various modes of constructing them. The slightest acquaintance with sanitary science will suffice to show that it is everybody's business, since every inhabitant of a country must breathe the air of that country, and since that air is rendered wholesome or pernicious by the system of sewerage in use. Besides, they who have the control of public affairs are urged to the performance of their duty by the force of public opinion, which, as it is enlightened or otherwise, will be beneficial or mischievous in its influence.

It forms consequently a part of the education of the people, to be acquainted with all those laws which regulate the condition of public health. In looking back along the pages of history, we meet with the records of a fearful succession of plagues and pestilences, which the chroniclers record roughly, without attempting to assign their causes, or describe the remedies made use of. They only relate, with an exaggeration pardonable because it was inspired by fear, that the living were scarcely sufficient in number to bury the dead.

The explanation of these terrible facts is to be found in the defective sanitary arrangements of those ages.

The activity of the principle of population was checked by ignorance; fens and marshes were left undrained, to send up their pestilential exhalations; forests were not ventilated by the removal of the undergrowth; and even towns and cities, the habitations of men, were permitted to abound with sources of disease and death. In many cities of the Continent, dust, decayed vegetables, and offal, accumulating in vast heaps, obstructed the streets, blocked up the avenues of market-places, and diffused the most noisome effluvia through the atmosphere. In remoter ages, Thebes, Babylon, Athens, Rome, and Syracuse swarmed with healthy populations; and therefore we may be certain the inhabitants possessed all the knowledge necessary to ensure health. But knowledge is not always able to provide for its own continuance. Time and chance happen to all men. On the ruins of those mighty cities, whose substructions still exist to prove the sanitary science of those who dwelt in them, we now find troops of squalid savages, vegetating in the midst of filth which they are too indolent to clear away.

In many parts of modern Europe, in the midst of splendid architecture, it is sickening to walk the streets before breakfast. Paris is perfectly hideous to early risers; and every great city of France, in proportion to its extent, is a repetition of the capital. Many

German towns—Cologne for example—lie for ever steeped in a fetid atmosphere, which affects travellers like ipecacuanha.

We may fairly congratulate ourselves, therefore, on having made a little more progress than our neighbours, though we have still a great deal to learn, and much more to put in practice. Our active reformers are occasionally disposed to speak contemptuously of books, because they behold men in possession of boundless libraries, who yet do little or nothing towards purifying the air they breathe; but we may as well despise knowledge as the means of knowledge, nay, we may even disdain the atmosphere, because it will not keep itself pure. Books, like everything else, are beneficial or otherwise as they are used. A man may pore over Petrarca's sonnets, or Metastasio's operas, to the neglect of his drains; but the fault is neither in the operas nor in the sonnets. There is no study or occupation by which we may not be so completely absorbed as to neglect others equally important.

Regarded as a habitation for man, London must, I think, be admitted to be the first city in the world. Its architecture is inferior to that of Paris; its site will bear no comparison for beauty with that of Constantinople, Naples, or even Palermo; but, looking below as well as above the ground, and taking all the comforts and conveniences of life into account, it is immensely superior to them all. The average length of human life is longer, nearly by one-third, than in any one of those cities, while the health and strength of the population are greater in a still more remarkable degree. Nevertheless even here it is impossible to walk the streets during the prevalence of certain winds, and immediately before rain, without being made sensible of immense defects in our subterranean architecture. Even above-ground it would not be difficult to point out numerous proofs of ignorance or negligence. In parts of London there are streets in which carts sink up to the axletree in abominable filth, while the whole neighbourhood is infested with deleterious gases.

We have consequently, as a nation, very much to learn in this respect. Again, in the building of houses for the poor, though a beginning of improvement has been made in various parts of the country, we have, upon the whole, scarcely advanced beyond the practice of the middle ages. In remote districts we hear of peasants constructing huts for themselves and their wives, not exceeding an ordinary table in height, without window or chimney, and having, instead of a door, merely a hole to creep in through, like the entrance to the lair of a wild beast.

Above this class of dens there is another, far more numerous, in which the inmates can stand upright, though they have no floor but the common earth, no escape for the smoke but what the poor peasants call a tout-hole, that is, a round aperture in a corner of the roof, which may be covered during rainy weather with a large stone. In these habitations there is no division of rooms; but the whole family, pigs and all, live together, to the great detriment of decorum, morals, and health.

The first step towards introducing a change in this state of things, will be to diffuse a knowledge of existing evils. Thousands who live in spacious houses, warmed, ventilated, carpeted, filled with gorgeous furniture, adorned with silken hangings, pictures, statues, and engraved gems, can scarcely be made to believe that immense multitudes of their fellow-creatures, whom nature intended to be in every way their equals, lead their whole lives in habitations inferior to many pig-styes. It will be one object of the National Association to enlighten them on this point. They will thus be enabled to perceive one of the greatest obstacles in the way of education. Nothing short of a miracle could persuade extensive knowledge to take up its abode in hovels such as I have described. The man's mind is dwarfed and cramped by the narrow dimensions of his dwelling. Like his body, it requires more room. The first lesson to be taught the poor is self-respect, which they can never entertain, or even be made to comprehend, until they are delivered from those depressing and degrading associations which naturally, I may say necessarily, cling to the dens in which they have hitherto been confined.

Every convert to the new system may be looked upon as the trophy of a victory gained over barbarism. In this process we have a long way to travel before we reach the poor; but the stone has been thrown into the pool, the circle is enlarging, and by degrees will embrace the whole empire. At present however we must confine our hopes, and even our operations, to those bordering immediately upon the centre of activity. Even Parliament, it is said, is not yet sufficiently alive to the importance of that knowledge which regards the promotion of public health. It admits, as a general theorem, that education is good; but as a body it does not yet distinctly comprehend to what extent it is good, or how it may be most effectually diffused.

The stern scientific man will perhaps scorn the aid of fancy and imagination in his endeavours to improve the condition of the people; but, even on a subject like this, it may be prudent to unite, as far as possible, the agreeable with the useful. Among the means of commanding public attention would be a museum of cottage architecture, gardening, and domestic economy. In this might be collected models of all kinds of houses for town and country, showing the best means of economizing space and promoting comfort.

In many old rustic houses in the remoter provinces, where houses are built with stone, you find large convenient niches, in the thickness of the wall, constructed in a picturesque shape, and supplied with shelves. These serve instead of so many pieces of furniture, and are admirably calculated to hold articles which need to be kept cool. Together with the cottage there might be the plan of a garden, with drawings of all the plants, fruit-trees, and flowers, the cultivation of which would be within a peasant's reach. In many parts of England, every labourer's dwelling might be accompanied by colonies of bees, whose honey and wax would prove a source of considerable profit. Mead also, a favourite drink of our ancestors, could easily be made, and supply the family with a wholesome and delicious drink through a large portion of the year.

Where there exists right of common, the poor often keep cows, pigs, and poultry; and it would certainly

be desirable to extend the taste for this kind of possessions, by familiarizing the humbler classes with all
those means by which they may be turned to the best
account. This may not deserve to be reckoned among
the social sciences; but real philosophers think nothing beneath their attention, which is calculated to
promote the welfare of their fellow-creatures. Swift
maintains, that he who causes two blades of grass to
grow, where only one blade grew before, is a benefac-
tor to the human race; and it may be affirmed with
equal truth, that he belongs to the same exalted class
of men, who introduces one single new article of comfort into the dwellings of the poor. Here education
borders upon the grand mission of Providence, diffusing light and blessing into the forlorn places of the
earth; and the day will assuredly come, when the
leaders in this great revolution will take their places,
even before statesmen and warriors, in the temple of
everlasting fame.

CHAPTER XXV.

TENDENCY OF CIVILIZATION.

Pre-eminence of Physical Enjoyment.—What things are first sacrificed in Difficulties.—Spiritualism and Materialism.—Ideas, and the Goods of Fortune.—Slaves of Property.—Great Aim of Education.—Vice of Imitation.—Extravagance the Parent of Vice.—Servants and Ladies.—Female Savages.—Sumptuary Laws.—Philosophy of Mandeville.—The Monastic Orders.—When Education becomes Useful.—Causes of National Degeneracy.—Example of the Roman Empire.—Selfishness overwhelms Patriotism.—Worship of Money.—Modern Slavery.—Evils of a too Dense Population.—Peopling the Wildernesses.—Integrity alone honourable.—The Family and the State. — What Knowledge raises the Poor.—Liberty and Arms.—Crowning Study, Religion.

TAKEN altogether, it is the tendency of modern systems of education to materialize the people. This also is the tendency of our civilization itself. Confessedly or secretly, we set up physical enjoyment as the aim of life, and sacrifice everything to that. To become thoroughly convinced of this, it is only necessary to consider what it is that people do, when, through the action of public affairs, there comes any great strain upon their fortunes. Do they show by their conduct that they prefer the good of the mind and the soul to the good of the body? Do they retrench the luxuries of the table, of their wardrobes, of their habitations, in the first place, and afterwards those luxuries of the understanding and imagination which are the furthest removed from sense.

When the necessity for retrenchment arrives, people commonly take the first step by relinquishing for the time their acquaintance with literature and the fine arts, and then the education of their children. These are suffered to stay at home, vegetating in idleness, and contracting vicious habits, while their wine-cellar continues to be filled, and all the material enjoyments of the family go on as before.

If the spiritual principle prevailed over the material, our proceedings would be exactly the reverse. What are called the common necessaries of life must undoubtedly be provided in the first case, because without them existence itself becomes impossible. But, these conditions having been fulfilled, I maintain that it is better for all men, even the very poorest, to fill their minds with ideas and moral principles and religious feelings, than to accumulate any kind or amount of property. The goods of fortune, without these ideas, habits, and principles, are beyond description unstable; but when a man has a firm, well-disciplined mind, he knows how to use and keep what he has. It is only the loose, frivolous, vulgar class of minds that go on perpetually grasping after new possessions, which they can neither employ nor enjoy, to which they become slaves more imbecile and pitiable than they who are slaves to masters of their own species.

The great aim of education should be to check this spirit, now hurrying modern nations into the track which conducted all previous communities to effeminacy and ruin.

In England the prevailing vice is imitation; the nobles imitate the Queen, the gentry imitate the nobles, and in general all classes strive to vie with and be mistaken for those above them in the social scale. This leads to that extravagance in houses, furniture, equipages, dress, ornaments, and style of living, which begets more than half the vices of which philosophers and moralists complain. They who write or converse about the education of the people, are often very severe upon all indications of this vice in poor persons. Ladies, for example, are extremely eloquent in denouncing the folly of cooks and housemaids who attempt to dress like their mistresses. But if ladies really wish poor girls to reform, they must begin by setting them an example. There is scarcely a young beauty in the land who would not, if she could, equal the Queen herself in pomp and splendour, in equipages, jewels, and dress.

The feeling, it may be said, is natural; but so perhaps are all other vices. The female savage is fonder of paint and feathers than the male, and the reason is to be discovered in the principles of human nature. We need not therefore seek to eradicate it, since it often leads to good; but we may and must seek to check and modify it, and direct it into the proper channels.

Many Governments, especially in former periods of the history of mankind, have attempted to accomplish this by sumptuary laws, regulating the dwellings, furniture, clothes, and even food, which should be possessed or consumed by the individuals of different classes. Against such laws, political economy would now vehemently exclaim.

Under certain disguises, the philosophy in fashion is the philosophy of Mandeville, which inculcates that private vices are public benefits. If we desire to maintain the high place we hold among the nations of the world, we must abjure this mode of thinking. It is better that the manufacturing system should receive a slight check, than that large classes of men and women should degrade themselves to obtain finery. But this result will never be brought about, unless by the united influence of religion, philosophy, and sound policy, until the classes who give the tone to public taste and opinion in these matters can be prevailed upon to change their tactics. If people will go gorgeously attired to teach moderation to the poor, they may rely upon it they will fail in their mission.

The members of the monastic orders thoroughly understood this, when they laid aside all splendour of apparel, and presented themselves with bare head and bare feet, clad in a haircloth sack, with a common rope for a girdle about their loins, to inculcate upon the poor the wisdom and the necessity of being contented with little; they could point to themselves by way of illustration. They could say, "We do not ask you to live like us, to make the sacrifices which we make, to refrain as we refrain from all the luxuries and enjoyments of the world; we only desire to persuade you to use them with reserve and moderation, and not to aim at distinguishing yourselves by going beyond your neighbours in these matters."·

Without pretending to advocate this theory, I still maintain that education is of little use unless it enables men to bring their conduct into something like conformity with reason. In old and luxurious communities, it is difficult to restrain the tendency towards extravagance; all readers of history are familiar with the efforts made by philosophers, whether they wrote in verse or prose, to arrest the Roman people in their headlong descent towards political extinction. They inveighed against the vices of the age, they pointed out criminals by name, they drew glowing and fascinating pictures of the barbarous populations which surrounded them, in order, if possible, to shame their countrymen into virtue ; but all was of no avail: the majority had adopted the conviction that it is every man's duty to look after himself, and not after the interest of the community ; and therefore all the arguments that could be drawn from the inexhaustible armoury of eloquence, failed to subdue that absorbing selfishness which had found its way into every heart, and eaten up the very germs of virtue. Marriage fell into discredit, children lost all reverence for their parents, luxury and effeminacy infected all mankind like a pestilence ; and money, the only instrument that could procure men what they desired, was sought after by every modification of crime.

If we suffer the contagion of similar sentiments to be diffused among us, we shall inevitably be overwhelmed by the same catastrophe.

One vast and pernicious fallacy, which prevails among us, is that of maintaining that slavery does not exist in modern society. It it true that civilization has deprived it of some of its most odious characteristics; but the poor, by whatsoever name we may choose to designate them, are still in the condition of servitude. They do not belong to this or that individual, but they are the slaves of the community. It is circumstances now, and not particular classes of men, that keep them in their place, constrain them to toil incessantly, to feed on scanty food, to be immersed in ignorance, to be incapable of going far from the place of their birth, or rising, except by something like a miracle, from their social degradation and wretchedness. To better the condition of this servile class is one of the great objects of the present generation, and a blessing will rest on every man who earnestly co-operates in the good work.

The first and great step towards elevating the poor is to thin their numbers. A dense population is necessarily a debased population; not that by any mysterious process men corrupt each other by crowding in great numbers together, but that there are too many competitors for the amount of work required to be done. First they bid below each other for the privilege of being allowed to toil; and when they cannot

even thus obtain enough to keep soul and body together, they necessarily betake themselves to dishonesty; for, preach as you please, men will always believe that they must live some way or another.

Well then, thin the population, not by any vicious
contrivances for checking it, but by opening up a
broad channel, by which it may flow out into the
uninhabited parts of the empire. Let it not however
flow forth according as chance may direct, but be
instructed, and prepared, and imbued with good sound
English principles, that it may bear along with it the
seeds of all those virtues which have made our nation
great. As far as education can affect the mind, let
the belief be diffused, that men are respectable and
honourable, not through any mysterious charm of
descent, but according as they conduct themselves in
life. If they are upright, if they are sincere, if they
entertain great sentiments, if they love their families
and their country, and if they are ready at all times
to make sacrifices of self for both, then they are
noble by nature, whatever the Heralds' College may
say. England owes its greatest glory to the indomitable energy, the courage, the integrity and boundless enterprise of its people; and every individual of
the empire must be filled by the persuasion that he
has a double life to live,—first as the member of a

family, and second as the citizen of a great State, to which he is indebted, next after God, for the highest distinction a man can enjoy.

The poor, at present, cannot be said to have risen to this level. They obey laws which they have no share in making, they pay taxes imposed on them, whether they will or not, by the representatives of other classes; and therefore, under a different name, they belong to the servile class. It is the object of the friends of education to remove from us as a people this stigma, which we have borne much too long. It is nothing to us that nearly all the other nations of Europe are in a state of bondage. It is the characteristic of our race never to rest content with anything less than complete freedom, which no nation can enjoy until it is in the possession of knowledge,—not a knowledge of arts and sciences, but the knowledge of what is due to every member of the human family as such.

It is well to be acquainted with the processes of industry, with manufactures, with commerce, with navigation; it is well not to be ignorant of the steam-engine, the electric-telegraph, or the printing-press; but it is abdicating altogether the character of an Englishman, not to be familiar with that which forms the peculiar pride of our race,—political liberty, and the use of those arms by which our forefathers acquired and defended it. Among the Athenians every citizen was taught to read and to swim; and every Englishman should be taught the value of his freedom, and the use of arms, by which alone it can be defended against the world.

There is another thing of still higher import, which should be every man's study, whether slave or free. I mean Religion, or the sum of those duties which we owe to our Creator. Without this there is no dignity, or freedom, or greatness of spirit. The man who is destitute of religion has forfeited the highest distinction of his nature, and degraded himself to the level of the inferior animals, from which we are chiefly distinguished by our knowledge of the God that made us. A Roman poet observes that man is the only creature formed with a countenance looking towards the skies, to intimate whence he came, and whither he must ultimately go. All other creatures have their faces turned towards the earth, which is to bound their aspirations and their hopes, while, in the language of the spirits in Milton,

> "By our own proper motion we ascend ;
> Descent and fall, to us is adverse."

Every sentiment which will not harmonize with this conviction, should be expelled like poison from the soul. Without it, we cannot bear the ills of life in a calm and dignified manner; but with it, there is nothing which the mind finds it difficult to subdue. Here we have the sheet-anchor of the English people, their Palladium, their sacred fire, which converts the poorest hearth of the poorest hovel into a great altar, on which God does not disdain to hold converse with man. We must introduce this belief into every form of education, not in a sectarian spirit, but in a great catholic sense, calculated to disperse and obliterate the prejudices which separate man from man. With this conviction the Legislature, it is to be hoped, will shortly approach the momentous subject of Education, not with reference to the poor only, but to all classes. Our system of instruction still falls very far short of what it ought to be, considering the advantages we enjoy, and the great force and capacity of the minds with which nature has gifted us.

I throw this volume, as the widow threw her mite, into the general treasury, not, of course, without the hope that it may be productive of some good; so that the object is certainly laudable, whatever may be thought of the performance itself.

INDEX.

—◆—

Ability, how far the gift of Nature, 281.
Accomplishments, fatal to the poor, 111.
Addison, his mental idiosyncrasies, 29; his works translated into Bengalee, 191.
Affection, innate, 109.
Affections, discipline of, 107; regulation of, 108.
Agriculture, animals employed in, 177; its ancillary sciences, 177.
Agricultural schools, 168; should be kept open in the evening, 183.
All-hallows Eve, bead-roll of, 27.
Alphabet, characters of, 78.
Alps, of the physical and intellectual world, 87; plants and flowers of, 179.
Amusements, suitable, needed by the people, 210.
Ancestors, English, their pride and valour, 166.
Ancients, ideas of, found in modern literature, 91; their healthy populations, 295.
Anecdote of a French physician, 251; of a lady, 59; of a peasant boy, 142.
Animals, what, the companions of man, 78.
Apparatus, for imparting knowledge, 45; of repression, rendered needless by knowledge, 162.
Apparitions, seen at night by a lady, 26.
Arab chief, anecdote of, 229; peasants, educated by the story-tellers, 121; peasant, anecdote of, 122.
Arabian traveller, his curious mistake, 237.
Architecture, its effect upon the mind, 221.
Aristocratic lecturers, their numerous advantages, 126.
Aristotle, saying of, 255.
Arms, a knowledge of the use of, necessary to freedom, 311.
Art, uneducated persons stunned by exhibitions of, 237; true object of, 239; the various delights it affords, 241.
Artists, peculiarity of their lives, 239.
Arts, use of, in education, 233.
Asheyr, beautiful silk of, 180; where found, 181.
Asiatic empire, growth of, 193; diffusion of knowledge in, 193; social movement in, 135.
Astronomy, grand prospects which it opens up to the mind, 64.
Athenians, their artistic taste, 242; elements of their education, 311.

Burke, his ideas on infant labour, 181.

Burns and Chatterton, 73.

Business men, character of their studies, 281.

Cæsar, his remark on Sylla, 254.

Calcutta, state of education at, 137.

Castlereagh, Lord, his Fire Spirit, 24.

Catholic hierarchy, 45.

Catholic priest, his defence of Latin, 232.

Causes of phenomena unknown, 65.

Caverns exchanged for houses, 77.

Cecil, Lord Robert, agrees with Rousseau, 108 ; his notions of a peasant, 169 ; his picture of savages, 226 ; his paradox on school teaching, 108 ; reasons in a circle, 109 ; satisfied with the progress of education, 3.

Charity schools, how to render needless, 166.

Charles V., saying of, 250.

Chatelain, Le Chevalier de, his translation of Chaucer, 53.

Chaucer, obstacles to his popularity, 53 ; variety of, 54.

Cheap books, when serviceable, 134.

Childhood, effects of instruction given in, 183.

Children, false ideas of, 5 ; importance of their first impressions, 130 ; criminal, number of, 18 ; of farmers and labourers, 184 ; of the poor, their sad advantages, 112.

Christ, inquiries of children concerning, 100 ; His ministry in Palestine, 48.

Christian country, state of children in, 99.

Christianity, growth of, how to be accelerated, 48 ; universally recognized, 99.

Church, not open for all, 46 ; of England, richest in the world, 45.

Civilization, its usual tendency, 167 ; small beginnings of, 77, 302.

Clairon, Mademoiselle, anecdote of, 219.

Classes, their reciprocal influence, 222 ; intercourse of, 226.

Classical literature, 39.

Claude Lorraine, and other landscape painters, 242.

Clergy, examples of apostolic zeal among, 231 ; their great services in the cause of education, 94 ; change needed in their training, 48 ; numbers of, 45 ; their intercourse with the poor, 230 ; their wish to benefit the poor, 264 ; their claim to educate youth, 94.

Clergymen, their wives and daughters, 118.

Cobden, Mr., a friend to popular education, 3.

Coffin borne by spirits, 26.

Collections of works of art, 234.

Cologne, its fœtid atmosphere, 296.

Colonies, contrasted with workhouses, 205 ; correct ideas of, 187 ; facility of intercourse, 186 ; false ideas of, common, 206 ; objections of the poor to, 187.

Comic histories and travels, 80.

Common, right of, 300.

Common sense, its influence, 102.

Conduct, good and bad, 70.

Conquest, what leads to it, 186 ; responsibilities of, 9.

England, 175; its greatest re-
commendation, 240.
Language, figurative among the
poor, 225; formation of, 78;
study of discouraged by Lord
Stanley, 246.
Latin books superseded by English, 147.
Laws affected by education, 271;
importance of the study of,
282; immense influence of,
282.
Lawyers, their peculiar terminology, 283.
Lecturers, condemned by various
noblemen, 127; their characteristics, 127; their importance
overrated, 126.
Lectures, where useful, 128.
Legislature, perplexed by varieties of opinion, 4.
Lending libraries, their effects on
the female poor, 134.
Lesser poets, their works, 56.
License of book-hawkers, 141.
Life, its three divisions, 133;
what it is that supports it,
98.
Light writers find light readers,
80.
Literature improved by diffusion,
146; loved for its own sake,
155; should be pervaded by a
religious spirit, 50; true character of its style, 147; of
England abounds in poetry.
52.
Literature and art, their reciprocal influence, 238; of England
breathe of the field, 174; post-
poned to luxury, 303.
Love of dress to be regulated,
not eradicated, 305.
London, longevity in, 297; heal-
thiest of great cities, 296; still
needs improvement, 297; treasures of art in, 235.

Luxury, the passion for, how to
be checked, 306.
Lycurgus imitated by Napoleon,
160.

Malefactors, dens of, 17.
Male teachers, objected to at
Agra, 136.
Manchester, bishop of, 244; Art
Exhibition at, anecdotes of,
236.
Man, a religious animal, 86; his
multiplied relations, 310; how
distinguished from inferior animals, 311; our duty towards,
105.
Mandeville, his philosophy fa-
shionable, 305.
Manufacturers, their efforts for
the improvement of taste, 234;
their sacrifices for education,
234.
Maps, coloured ethnologically,
183; illustrating the distribution of religions, 84; illustrating the distribution of animals and plants, 85.
Marlow and the other dramatists, 55.
Martineau, Miss F., her school
at Norwich, 112.
Material civilization precedes
mental, 275.
Mathematical students, 226.
Maurice, Rev. Mr., his college,
136; his views on female education, 137.
Mead, a favourite drink of our
ancestors, 300.
Meadows, creation of, 77.
Mechanics' Institutes, collective
members of, 214; defective organization of, 259; not suited
to women, 124; number of,
7; supposed to have failed,
208; students of foreign languages in, 255.

rests and fisheries of, 203;
cheapness of land in, 203; picturesque interior, 203.
New language, acquisition of, 256.
Newspapers, histories of the
hour, 63; the people's best instructors, 62.
New Zealand, ludicrous objections to, 194.
Noblemen, their lectures, 223.
North countrymen, shrewdness
of, 228.
Northern nations, their taste in
art, 243.
Northumberland, Duke of, his
gallery, 235.
Nottinghamshire, scarcity of
teachers in, 182.
Novel, a domestic epic, 60; ini-
mical to the drama, 60; prejudice against, 59; what it is,
59.
Noxious insects extirpated, 178.
Nubians, their taste for botany,
180.
Nubia, substitute for coffee in,
180.

Ocean, its inhabitants, 204.
Old country-houses, their conve-
niences, 300.
Old women, swimming of, 31.
Oneiromancy, interpretation of
dreams, 35.
Opportunity, its force, 72.
Opulent, their leisure hours, 133.
Orange and willow girls, 122.
Orientals, lower classes of, 120.
Oriental stories, instruction con-
veyed by, 120.
Ottoman empire, peasants of,
227.
Our ancestors, their domestic
virtues, 115.
Our language, means of im-
proving, 224.
Our literature, its character, 62.

Our Puritan ancestors, their
Spartan spirit, 96.
Outlying provinces, their inter-
esting character, 267.

Pakington, the Right Hon. Sir
John, debate on his motion,
102; his anecdote of a vagrant boy, 196; his earnestness
of purpose, 285; a strenuous
advocate of popular instruction, 3; his name linked with
the cause of education, 285;
people's friend, not their flatterer, 285; his speech at Manchester, 158; the great advocate of education, 280.
Palmerston, Lord, his rational
views, 66; his recommenda-
tion of poetry, 52; his speech
at Manchester, 292; his speech
in the Free Trade Hall, 22.
Pandemonium of civilization, 15.
Paradise Lost, anecdote of, 148;
its great popularity, 147.
Parents, cruelty of, 16.
Parisian women, 122.
Paris, its want of cleanliness,
295; its immorality, 160; publication committee of, 141.
Parliament, its indifference, 299;
various theories of, 287.
Parochial antiquities, 149.
Patricians of intellect, 76.
Peasantry, their books, 264; of
France, incurious, 179; schools
for, 174; their duties and
wants, 184.
Peasants, their language and
manners, 228; children, their
education, 181; ignorance of,
168; in free and despotic
states, 228.
Pedantry, old and new, 248.
Peel, Sir Robert, his comic lec-
ture, 223.
Penelope, her suitors, 25.

Utility not necessarily attractive, 149.

Vanity, pivot of French education, 160; the mother of irreligion, 97.
Various districts, their natural history, 264.
Volney, paradox of, 95.
Voltaire, life of Charles XII., 150.

Wages, how to be increased, 267.
Want of instruction, effects of, 119.
Warlike amusements, their interest, 216.
Wealth, how generated, 281.
Wellington, Duke of, Apsley House, 235.
White, 'Natural History of Selborne,' 264.
Wilderness, sanctified by religion, 207.
Will, force of, 220.
William the Norman, his indifference, 61.
Wisdom in verse, 58.
Witchcraft, belief in, hardens the heart, 30; ingenious defence of, 29; disclosures respecting, 23.
Witches on horseback, 28.
Wives, prudent and imprudent, 113.
Women, by what motives influenced, 134; defective education of, in Scotland, 131; difficulties attending their emigration, 198; difficulty of teaching them, 122; lectures suited to, 128; Institutes for their use, 125; mothers of their children's minds, 129; nature of their duties, 133;

neatness of, 113; no adequate provisions for teaching, 130; of England not fairly treated, 122; of Greece, obstacles to teaching, 137; of the people, instruction of, 132; partial to lectures, 128; schools for, at Agra, 135; superior in some countries to men, 122; their education by books, 134; character of their education, 129; importance of instructing them, 111; their primary education defective, 128; training, 134; unsuitable studies, 130.
World, judgment of, formed in darkness, 89; knowledge of, how acquired, 253; of knowledge, its divisions, 67.
Workhouses, how to be cleared out, 196.
Working-classes, false notions respecting, 209; not antiquarians, 265; studying Greek and Latin, 248; their taste for fiction, 217; their comforts and recreations, 211.
Working-man, limits of his knowledge, 66; men, their style of reading, 79; women, classes of, 130; Women's College in London, 130.
Worship based on love, 69; necessary to man, 86.
Work enough for all, 67.
Works of Art, mysterious, in Egypt and Nubia, 238.

Youth of Ireland, imperfect education of, 172.

Zeal and charity, their fruits among the poor, 231.

THE END.